ALMA AND ABINADI

ALMA AND ABINADI

Mark E. Petersen

Deseret Book Company
Salt Lake City, Utah

This book is not an official Church publication, nor has it been written by assignment or request of the First Presidency. Therefore, the views expressed therein do not necessarily represent the official position of the Church. The author, and he alone, is responsible for the contents.

CONTENTS

Behold I say unto you, that whosoever has heard the words of the prophets, yea, all the holy prophets who have prophesied concerning the coming of the Lord—I say unto you, that all those who have hearkened unto their words, and believed that the Lord would redeem his people, and have looked forward to that day for a remission of their sins, I say unto you, that these are his seed, or they are the heirs of the kingdom of God.

For these are they whose sins he has borne; these are they for whom he has died, to redeem them from their transgression. And now, are they not his seed?

But behold, and fear, and tremble before God, for ye ought to tremble; for the Lord redeemeth none such that rebel against him and die in their sins; yea, even all those that have perished in their sins ever since the world began, that have wilfully rebelled against God, that have known the commandments of God, and would not keep them; these are they that have no part in the first resurrection.

—Abinadi, in Mosiah 15:11-12, 26

Chapter 1

ANOTHER "THREE WITNESSES"

Nearly two centuries before Christ, three of his mightiest witnesses arose in ancient America.

Two came out of a period of gross iniquity that involved them deeply; yet they reached spiritual heights seldom known by men. Very much like Saul of Tarsus, they turned from being enemies of Jesus to becoming devoted advocates.

The third was burned at the stake for his testimony.

Each foretold the Savior's birth into mortality and the Atonement he would accomplish for all mankind. Their names and labors cannot be separated, for their ministries were closely intertwined.

Their testimonies were unshakable and stand even today as beacon lights to all generations of men. And who were they?

Two were named Alma—father and son, both of them towers of faith and devotion.

The other was Abinadi, a fearless champion and martyr for the word of God, an inspired herald of the expected Messiah.

In ancient America these three fully identified the Lord as the Only Begotten Son of God and taught that his name would be Jesus Christ. Four hundred years earlier the Lord revealed to the prophet Nephi, also in America, details of the mission of Jesus, including his virgin birth and crucifixion. The Almas and Abinadi built on Nephi's foundation. They explained the Atonement in detail, stressed the resurrection of the dead, and made it clear that while all who die will be raised from their graves, salvation from sin will come only to those who accept and obey the gospel.

The people of their day lived under the law of Moses as well as the gospel, and the relationship of the two was explained. These men taught that Christ, as the Law-Giver himself, would also fulfill the law when he came in mortality; in its place he would provide a higher spirituality, not based on the routine performance of the rites of the law, but on the elevation of the soul. Thereby mankind could become "even as I am," to use the Savior's words.

The way to peace and prosperity was pointed out by these three prophets, and always it was the way of Christ. Said one of them:

"For I say unto you that whatsoever is good cometh from God, and whatsoever is evil cometh from the devil.

"Therefore, if a man bringeth forth good works he hear-keneth unto the voice of the good shepherd, and he doth follow him; but whosoever bringeth forth evil works, the same becometh a child of the devil, for he hearkeneth unto his voice, and doth follow him. And whosoever doeth this must receive his wages of him; therefore, for his wages he receiveth death, as to things pertaining unto righteousness, being dead unto all good works.

"And now, my brethren, I would that ye should hear me, for I speak in the energy of my soul; for behold, I have spoken unto you plainly that ye cannot err, or have spoken according to the commandments of God. For I am called to speak after this manner, according to the holy order of God, which is in Christ Jesus; yea, I am commanded to stand and testify unto this people the things which have been spoken by our fathers concerning the things which are to come.

"And this is not all. Do ye not suppose that I know of these things myself? Behold, I testify unto you that I do know that these things whereof I have spoken are true. And how do ye suppose that I know of their surety? Behold, I say unto you they are made known unto me by the Holy Spirit of God. Behold, I have fasted and prayed many days that I might know these things of myself. And now I do know of myself that they are true; for the Lord God hath made them manifest unto me by his Holy Spirit; and this is the spirit of revelation which is in me.

"And moreover, I say unto you that it has thus been revealed unto me, that the words which have been spoken by our fathers are true, even so according to the spirit of prophecy which is in me, which is also by the manifestation of the Spirit of God.

"I say unto you, that I know of myself that whatsoever I shall say unto you, concerning that which is to come, is true; and I say unto you, that I know that Jesus Christ shall come, yea, the Son, the Only Begotten of the Father, full of grace, and mercy, and truth. And behold, it is he that cometh to take away the sins of the world, yea, the sins of every man who steadfastly believeth on his name." (Alma 5:40-48.)

Chapter 2

THEIR BEGINNING

The ministry of these three prophets actually arose out of the reign of the wicked King Noah, who lived about 160 B.C.

Noah ruled a colony living apart from the main body of Nephites in the area of Zarahemla. His little kingdom was many days' journey into the wilderness in a region of the land of Nephi that was known as Lehi-Nephi.

Noah's father, a righteous man named Zeniff, led the colony away from Zarahemla. When he arrived in the land of Nephi, he found it occupied by the Lamanites. He entered into a treaty with the king of the Lamanites, who moved his own people out and allowed Zeniff to take it over. This colony enjoyed peace for twelve years, and the people chose Zeniff as their king. He taught them righteousness, for he was devout, and they lived according to the commandments of the Lord.

The king of the Lamanites, whose name was Laban, was a crafty man. After the people of Zeniff became well established and began to prosper, he demanded tribute from them up to one-half of all their crops, their flocks, and their precious things. This brought on a war that was won by the Nephites. Another period of peace prevailed, this time for twenty-two years, but then the Lamanites renewed their attacks. Again Zeniff and his people fought "in the strength of the Lord" and drove the Lamanites away.

Zeniff by this time had become an old man, and he wished to relinquish his leadership of the growing colony. He bestowed the crown upon his son Noah, who turned against God and began to lead his people into debauchery and degradation.

King Noah "did not keep the commandments of God, but

he did walk after the desires of his own heart. And he had many wives and concubines. And he did cause his people to commit sin, and do that which was abominable in the sight of the Lord. Yea, and they did commit whoredoms and all manner of wickedness.

"And he laid a tax of one fifth part of all they possessed, a fifth part of their gold and of their silver, and a fifth part of their ziff, and of their copper, and of their brass and their iron; and a fifth part of their fatlings; and also a fifth part of all their grain.

"And all this did he take to support himself, and his wives and his concubines; and also his priests, and their wives and their concubines; thus he had changed the affairs of the kingdom. For he put down all the priests that had been consecrated by his father, and consecrated new ones in their stead, such as were lifted up in the pride of their hearts.

"Yea, and thus they were supported in their laziness, and in their idolatry, and in their whoredoms, by the taxes which king Noah had put upon his people; thus did the people labor exceedingly to support iniquity. Yea, and they also became idolatrous, because they were deceived by the vain and flattering words of the king and priests; for they did speak flattering things unto them.

"And it came to pass that king Noah built many elegant and spacious buildings; and he ornamented them with fine work of wood, and of all manner of precious things, of gold, and of silver, and of iron, and of brass, and of ziff, and of copper; and he also built him a spacious palace, and a throne in the midst thereof, all of which was of fine wood and was ornamented with gold and silver and with precious things.

"And it came to pass that he placed his heart upon his riches, and he spent his time in riotous living with his wives and his concubines; and so did also his priests spend their time with harlots.

"And it came to pass that he planted vineyards round about in the land; and he built winepresses, and made wine in abundance; and therefore he became a wine-bibber, and also his people." (Mosiah 11:2-9, 14-15.)

When Laban, king of the Lamanites, died, his son began to reign. The new king declared war on the Nephites but was badly defeated. The Nephites took many spoils in this war and rejoiced at their victory.

Since they had turned away from the Lord, through Noah's bad example, they gave God no credit for their success.

Chapter 3

ABINADI APPEARS

When King Noah's army returned from defeating the Lamanites, "they were lifted up in the pride of their hearts; they did boast in their own strength, saying that their fifty could stand against thousands of the Lamanites; and thus they did boast, and did delight in blood, and the shedding of the blood of their brethren, and this because of the wickedness of their king and priests." (Mosiah 11:19.)

But the Lord refused to bless them in their wickedness; instead, he rebuked them and called them to repentance.* Then there came among them a man whose name was Abinadi.

Who was Abinadi? The record indicates that he was one of the men who lived in the colony of King Noah, "a man among them." Although the king, along with many of his immediate followers, turned to wickedness, others remained loyal to the righteous teachings of Zeniff. Abinadi was one of them.

Abinadi came as a prophet of the Lord to call the people to repentance. He went among them and began to prophesy, saying: "Behold, thus saith the Lord, and thus hath he commanded me, saying, Go forth, and say unto this people, thus saith the Lord—Wo be unto this people, for I have seen their abominations, and their wickedness, and their whoredoms; and except they repent I will visit them in mine anger." (Mosiah 11:20.)

Note that Abinadi received a revelation from the Lord calling him to confront the king, and giving him instructions as to

---

*It is interesting to note that one of Noah's sons was a devout man who held true to the teachings of Zeniff in spite of his father's apostasy. This son was named Limhi. The record does not relate Limhi to either Alma or Abinadi. It is silent on his activity until after the death of Abinadi and the departure of Alma and his people. Limhi became the leader of the colony after his father, Noah, fled into the wilderness in fear of an approaching Lamanite army.

what he should say. His words were forceful: "Thus saith the Lord," he cried out, "and thus hath he commanded me," and then he quotes the language of the Lord.

God always directs his prophets. There was revelation in those days even as now. And so the Lord commanded Abinadi to give his warning, "Thus saith the Lord, Wo be unto this people."

This was revelation, and it was God's message to those people. Abinadi was but the instrument of communication. The language is in the first person, as the Lord himself addressed them. His words continue:

"Except they repent and turn to the Lord their God, behold, I will deliver them into the hands of their enemies; yea, and they shall be brought into bondage; and they shall be afflicted by the hand of their enemies. And it shall come to pass that they shall know that I am the Lord their God, and am a jealous God, visiting the iniquities of my people.

"And it shall come to pass that except this people repent and turn unto the Lord their God, they shall be brought into bondage; and none shall deliver them, except it be the Lord the Almighty God. Yea, and it shall come to pass that when they shall cry unto me I will be slow to hear their cries; yea, and I will suffer them that they be smitten by their enemies.

"And except they repent in sackcloth and ashes, and cry mightily to the Lord their God, I will not hear their prayers, neither will I deliver them out of their afflictions; and thus saith the Lord, and thus hath he commanded me."

This direct accusation angered the people. They attempted to seize Abinadi to kill him, but the Lord protected him, and he went into hiding. His assailants then reported the affair to King Noah.

"Now when King Noah had heard of the words which Abinadi had spoken unto the people, he was also wroth; and he said: Who is Abinadi, that I and my people should be judged of him, or who is the Lord, that shall bring upon my people such great affliction? I command you to bring Abinadi hither, that I may slay him, for he has said these things that he might stir up my people to anger one with another, and to raise contentions among my people; therefore I will slay him."

Abinadi's visit left the people more than ever entrenched in their sins. Their "hearts were hardened" against the words of the prophet as they searched for him that they might kill him.

"And king Noah hardened his heart against the word of the Lord, and he did not repent of his evil doings." (Mosiah 11: 21-29.)

Chapter 4

THE PROPHET RETURNS

Two years passed before Abinadi returned. This time he remained among the people, and the Lord permitted his arrest. This obviously was to provide opportunity for Abinadi to be taken into the royal court, where he could testify to the king and his courtiers.

Since Noah was surrounded by wicked priests, they too would hear Abinadi's warning. The prophet came by divine direction. His message was given to him by revelation. The Lord spoke to this humble but fearless prophet and told him: "Abinadi, go and prophesy unto this my people, for they have hardened their hearts against my words; they have repented not of their evil doings; therefore, I will visit them in my anger, yea, in my fierce anger will I visit them in their iniquities and abominations."

In his preaching the devoted prophet said:

"Yea, wo be unto this generation! And the Lord said unto me: Stretch forth thy hand and prophesy, saying: Thus saith the Lord, it shall come to pass that this generation, because of their iniquities, shall be brought into bondage, and shall be smitten on the cheek; yea, and shall be driven by men, and shall be slain; and the vultures of the air, and the dogs, yea, and the wild beasts, shall devour their flesh.

"And it shall come to pass that the life of king Noah shall be valued even as a garment in a hot furnace; for he shall know that I am the Lord. And it shall come to pass that I will smite this my people with sore afflictions, yea, with famine and with pestilence; and I will cause that they shall howl all the day long."

Abinadi described the afflictions that would come upon the

people if they failed to repent. He again spoke in the first person on behalf of the Lord, as if God himself was giving warning. The language of the Lord was:

"Yea, and I will cause that they shall have burdens lashed upon their backs; and they shall be driven before like a dumb ass. And it shall come to pass that I will send forth hail among them, and it shall smite them; and they shall also be smitten with the east wind; and insects shall pester their land also, and devour their grain. And they shall be smitten with a great pestilence—and all this will I do because of their iniquities and abominations.

"And it shall come to pass that except they repent I will utterly destroy them from off the face of the earth; yet they shall leave a record behind them, and I will preserve them for other nations which shall possess the land; yea, even this will I do that I may discover the abominations of this people to other nations."

The angry crowd took Abinadi immediately before the king, which apparently was part of the Lord's plan. The wicked monarch must be called to repentance. The Lord would leave him no excuse.

The people said to the king, "Behold we have brought a man before thee who has prophesied evil concerning thy people and saith that God will destroy them. And he also prophesieth evil concerning thy life, and saith that thy life shall be as a garment in a furnace of fire.

"And again, he saith that thou shalt be as a stalk, even as a dry stalk of the field, which is run over by the beasts and trodden under foot.

"And again, he saith thou shalt be as the blossoms of a thistle, which, when it is fully ripe, if the wind bloweth, it is driven forth upon the face of the land. And he pretendeth the Lord hath spoken it. And he saith all this shall come upon thee except thou repent, and this because of thine iniquities.

"And now, O king, what great evil hast thou done, or what

great sins have thy people committed, that we should be condemned of God or judged of this man?

"And now, O king, behold, we are guiltless, and thou, O king, hast not sinned; therefore, this man has lied concerning you, and he has prophesied in vain. And behold, we are strong, we shall not come into bondage, or be taken captive by our enemies; yea, and thou hast prospered in the land, and thou shalt also prosper. Behold, here is the man, we deliver him into thy hands; thou mayest do with him as seemeth thee good."

Noah immediately imprisoned Abinadi without even hearing him. But that was not the Lord's plan. The king personally must hear the warning. He called his wicked priests together to discuss the entire event and determine what should be done about it.

The priests wanted to question Abinadi in hopes of trapping him into making some statements damaging to himself.

"And they began to question him, that they might cross him, that thereby they might have wherewith to accuse him; but he answered them boldly, and withstood all their questions, yea, to their astonishment; for he did withstand them in all their questions, and did confound them in all their words."

Much of the discussion related to the law of Moses, which these wicked priests pretended to teach, but which they themselves violated, and which they allowed the people to ignore.

Abinadi said unto them, "Are you priests, and pretend to teach this people, and to understand the spirit of prophesying, and yet desire to know of me what these things mean?

"I say unto you, wo be unto you for perverting the ways of the Lord! For if ye understand these things ye have not taught them; therefore, ye have perverted the ways of the Lord. Ye have not applied your hearts to understanding; therefore, ye have not been wise. Therefore, what teach ye this people?"

They replied, "We teach the law of Moses."

Abinadi continued, "If ye teach the law of Moses why do ye not keep it? Why do ye set your hearts upon riches? Why do ye commit whoredoms and spend your strength with harlots, yea, and cause this people to commit sin, that the Lord has cause to send me to prophesy against this people, yea, even a great evil against this people?

"Know ye not that I speak the truth? Yea, ye know that I speak the truth; and you ought to tremble before God. And it shall come to pass that ye shall be smitten for your iniquities, for ye have said that ye teach the law of Moses. And what know ye concerning the law of Moses? Doth salvation come by the law of Moses? What say ye?"

They answered that salvation did come by the law of Moses.

Though the priests claimed that salvation came by the law of Moses itself, Abinadi corrected them and told them of Christ, through whom salvation truly comes. He pointed out that they were required to obey the law of Moses until Jesus should come in the flesh to fulfill it. Salvation is obtained only through Christ, he declared. His atonement provided it, not the performance of physical rituals. The Lord requires a righteous life, for no unclean thing may enter his presence. (Mosiah 12.)

Chapter 5

ABINADI'S DEFENSE

A lively discussion developed between Abinadi and the evil priests of King Noah. They tried to entrap him but failed. Inspired by the Holy Ghost, he resisted their every effort. He taught them the Ten Commandments and other laws of Moses, but particularly bore strong testimony of the mission of Christ.

Surprising as it may seem, one of the most significant things about Abinadi's teachings is that they parallel so closely the wording of the King James translation of the Bible. The Holy Land is a long way from America, and the ancient Americans lived many centuries before King James, but the striking similarity between the King James Version and Abinadi's words cannot be overlooked.

The King James Version was not prepared until the seventeenth century after Christ, whereas Abinadi ministered 150 years B.C., eighteen hundred years earlier. And yet, what he said confirms and sustains the accuracy of the King James Version in a most remarkable manner. It also testifies in no uncertain terms that the Lord guided the Prophet Joseph Smith, and that the publication of the Book of Mormon was nothing less than God's own work. Joseph was his inspired servant.

Some six hundred years before Christ, Lehi left Jerusalem at the command of the Lord. He was en route to what is now known as America, a land that the Almighty called choice above all other lands.

The Lord commanded Lehi to take with him the brass plates of Laban, which contained what had been written to that time of the ancient record that we know as the Old Testament. A priceless record, engraved on metal to resist the ravages of time, it would form for Lehi and his followers the basis of gospel teachings as well as the day-to-day education of his descendants. It was well known that people without written records lose their language as well as much of their culture, as was the case with the Mulekites.

The sons of Lehi obtained the plates from Laban, and the family took these sacred records with them to America. Their teachings were used for generations. In this manner the Ten Commandments and other writings from the Old Testament that were inscribed on the brass plates were available among the Nephites. Copies were made and distributed freely.

Abinadi did not have the brass plates themselves, since they were kept at the headquarters of the Church, probably in Zarahemla. But he had copies, and he was familiar with them. While he discoursed on the Ten Commandments with the priests of Noah, he quoted from those records. His quotations are nearly identical to the same passages as they appear in the King James Version of the Bible. For example, in the first commandment there are differences in only two words.

The King James Version reads: "I am the Lord thy God, which have brought thee out of the land of Egypt, out of the house of bondage. Thou shalt have no other gods before me." (Exodus 20:2-3.)

The quotation as given by Abinadi reads: "I am the Lord thy God who hath brought thee out of the land of Egypt, out of the house of bondage. Thou shalt have no other God before me." (Mosiah 12:34-35.)

The King James Version uses the word *which,* while Abinadi used *who;* and the word *God* is capitalized and used in the singular in Abinadi's words, as contrasted with the plural and lowercase word *gods* in the King James Version.

The second commandment as published in the Bible reads as follows: "Thou shalt not make unto thee any graven image, or any likeness of any thing that is in heaven above, or that is in

the earth beneath, or that is in the water under the earth."
(Exodus 20:4.)

Abinadi's version reads: "Thou shalt not make unto thee
any graven image, or any likeness of any thing in heaven above,
or things which are in the earth beneath." (Mosiah 12:36.)

Later in his speech he gave this same commandment with a
slight difference: "Thou shalt not make unto thee any graven
image, or any likeness of things which are in heaven above, or
which are in the earth beneath, or which are in the water under
the earth."

Then he continued, "Thou shalt not bow down thyself unto
them, nor serve them; for I the Lord thy God am a jealous God,
visiting the iniquities of the fathers upon the children, unto the
third and fourth generations of them that hate me; and showing
mercy unto thousands of them that love me and keep my commandments." (Mosiah 13:12-14.)

With the exception of two words, the two versions are identical in this passage also.

Anyone reading the Bible and the Book of Mormon may
make similar comparisons with the rest of the Ten Commandments and find that the two renderings are virtually the same.
This is a great testimony to the accuracy of the King James Version, for the Abinadi quotations are from the brass plates of
Laban, transferred to the gold plates of the Book of Mormon,
and then translated by the Prophet Joseph Smith through the use
of the Urim and Thummim. Hence they are correct.

In reading the fourteenth chapter of Mosiah, we see that
Abinadi quoted from the fifty-third chapter of Isaiah, one of the
grandest descriptions of the Savior's ministry ever written.
Abinadi's rendering is virtually identical to King James. Is this
not another testimony to the accuracy of the King James Version? Were not those translators of the seventeenth century inspired? Historians tell us that those English scholars undertook
their work in a spirit of prayer, with much fasting to reinforce
their perception. The Lord responded.

When Abinadi explained the passages relating to "how beautiful upon the mountains are the feet of him that bringeth good tidings," again we see a remarkable likeness between the two versions. (See Mosiah 15.)

This is representative of other Bible quotations in the Book of Mormon, and there are many of them. Not only was Isaiah quoted often in the Book of Mormon, but Malachi also—and he lived after Lehi left Jerusalem. The Savior gave his words directly to the Nephites—but they follow the King James text!

The most outstanding of all such examples is the Sermon on the Mount. There are few differences between the Book of Mormon version, given as the Savior delivered that sermon to the Nephites, and what appears in Matthew, chapters 5, 6, and 7, in the King James Version.

And be it remembered that the Book of Mormon passages were direct translations from the gold plates and given to us through the use of the Urim and Thummim. This great miracle is convincing testimony both to the Prophet Joseph Smith's calling with regard to the translation of the Book of Mormon and to the accuracy of the King James Version. Can we wonder then that The Church of Jesus Christ of Latter-day Saints has designated the King James Version as its official Bible?

Chapter 6

HIS STRONG TEACHINGS

The teachings of Abinadi, a revelation in and of themselves, fully reflect the writings of the other prophets, for the Lord is the same always. They are in full agreement with the teachings of the Prophet Joseph Smith.

Abinadi taught: "Little children also have eternal life." (Mosiah 15:25.)

How remarkably this statement corresponds with the teachings of the Prophet Joseph, such as those found in section 137 of the Doctrine and Covenants, the Prophet's Vision of the Celestial Kingdom:

"The heavens were opened upon us, and I beheld the celestial kingdom of God, and the glory thereof, whether in the body or out I cannot tell.

"I saw the transcendent beauty of the gate through which the heirs of that kingdom will enter, which was like unto circling flames of fire; also the blazing throne of God, whereon was seated the Father and the Son.

"I saw the beautiful streets of that kingdom, which had the appearance of being paved with gold.

"I saw Father Adam and Abraham; and my father and my mother; my brother Alvin, that has long since slept; and marveled how it was that he had obtained an inheritance in that kingdom, seeing that he had departed this life before the Lord had set his hand to gather Israel the second time, and had not been baptized for the remission of sins.

"Thus came the voice of the Lord unto me, saying: All who have died without a knowledge of this gospel, who would have received it if they had been permitted to tarry, shall be heirs of the celestial kingdom of God; also all that shall die henceforth without a knowledge of it, who would have received it with all their hearts, shall be heirs of that kingdom; for I, the Lord, will judge all men according to their works, according to the desire of their hearts.

"And I also beheld that all children who die before they arrive at the years of accountability are saved in the celestial kingdom of heaven."

After declaring the name of the Savior to the people of King Noah, Abinadi declared that salvation from sin comes only to the repentant who take upon them the name of Christ:

"Behold I say unto you, that whosoever has heard the words of the prophets, yea, all the holy prophets who have prophesied concerning the coming of the Lord—I say unto you, that all those who have hearkened unto their words, and believed that the Lord would redeem his people, and have looked forward to that day for a remission of their sins, I say unto you, that these are his seed, or they are the heirs of the kingdom of God. For these are they whose sins he has borne; these are they for whom he has died, to redeem them from their transgressions. And now, are they not his seed?" (Mosiah 15:11-12.)

In discussing the resurrection he said, "The bands of death shall be broken, and the Son reigneth, and hath power over the dead; therefore, he bringeth to pass the resurrection of the dead. And there cometh a resurrection, even a first resurrection; yea, even a resurrection of those that have been, and who are, and who shall be, even until the resurrection of Christ—for so shall he be called."

Some of the people evidently had questions in their minds as to whether people who lived before Christ would be resurrected at all, for Abinadi taught this beautiful doctrine:

"The resurrection of all the prophets, and all those that have believed in their words, or all those that have kept the commandments of God, shall come forth in the first resurrection; therefore, they are the first resurrection. They are raised to dwell with God who has redeemed them; thus they have eternal life through Christ, who has broken the bands of death. And these are those who have part in the first resurrection; and these are they that have died before Christ came, in their ignorance, not having salvation declared unto them. And thus the Lord bringeth about the restoration of these; and they have a part in the first resurrection, or have eternal life, being redeemed by the Lord."

Then he added:

"But behold, and fear, and tremble before God, for ye ought to tremble; for the Lord redeemeth none such that rebel against him and die in their sins; yea, even all those that have perished in their sins ever since the world began, that have wilfully rebelled against God, that have known the commandments of God, and would not keep them; these are they that have no part in the first resurrection.

"Therefore ought ye not to tremble? For salvation cometh to none such; for the Lord hath redeemed none such; yea, neither can the Lord redeem such; for he cannot deny himself; for he cannot deny justice when it has its claim.

"And now I say unto you that the time shall come that the salvation of the Lord shall be declared to every nation, kindred, tongue, and people." (Mosiah 15:20-28.)

Abinadi's further teachings concerning the Savior and the resurrection are an inspiration and great comfort to all:

"The time shall come when all shall see the salvation of the Lord; when every nation, kindred, tongue, and people shall see eye to eye and shall confess before God that his judgments are just.

"And then shall the wicked be cast out, and they shall have cause to howl, and weep, and wail, and gnash their teeth; and this because they would not hearken unto the voice of the Lord; therefore the Lord redeemeth them not. For they are carnal and devilish, and the devil has power over them; yea, even that old serpent that did beguile our first parents, which was the cause of their fall; which was the cause of all mankind becoming carnal, sensual, devilish, knowing evil from good, subjecting themselves to the devil.

"Thus all mankind were lost; and behold, they would have been endlessly lost were it not that God redeemed his people from their lost and fallen state.

"But remember that he that persists in his own carnal nature, and goes on in the ways of sin and rebellion against God, remaineth in his fallen state and the devil hath all power over him. Therefore, he is as though there was no redemption made, being an enemy to God; and also is the devil an enemy to God.

"And now if Christ had not come into the world, speaking of things to come as though they had already come, there could have been no redemption. And if Christ had not risen from the dead, or have broken the bands of death that the grave should have no victory, and that death should have no sting, there could have been no resurrection.

"But there is a resurrection, therefore the grave hath no victory, and the sting of death is swallowed up in Christ. He is the light and the life of the world; yea, a light that is endless, that can never be darkened; yea, and also a life which is endless, that there can be no more death.

"Even this mortal shall put on immortality, and this corruption shall put on incorruption, and shall be brought to stand before the bar of God, to be judged of him according to their works whether they be good or whether they be evil—if they be good, to the resurrection of endless life and happiness; and if they be evil, to the resurrection of endless damnation, being delivered up to the devil, who hath subjected them, which is damnation—having gone according to their own carnal wills and desires; having never called upon the Lord while the arms of mercy were extended towards them; for the arms of mercy were extended towards them, and they would not; they being warned of their iniquities and yet they would not depart from them; and they were commanded to repent and yet they would not repent.

"And now, ought ye not to tremble and repent of your sins, and remember that only in and through Christ ye can be saved?" (Mosiah 16:1-13.)

Chapter 7

ABINADI THE MARTYR

The teachings of Abinadi were rejected by the court of the wicked King Noah, who immediately commanded his priests to seize the prophet and put him to death.

But one of the priests had been converted by Abinadi's preaching. So deeply did he feel the power and spirit of the Lord's humble servant that he determined to try to save the prophet's life. Well aware of the evil against which Abinadi had warned them, this priest appealed to the king to release the prophet and let him "depart in peace."

The king became enraged at this. He not only condemned Abinadi to death, but also ejected the young priest from the palace and sent his soldiers out to slay him.

The young priest was Alma. He managed to escape and went into hiding. While secluded, he wrote all the words of the prophet.

Meanwhile, Abinadi was bound and thrown into prison, where he was held for three days while Noah counseled further with his priests as to what punishment should be given him. Then he was brought before the king, who said to him, "Abinadi, we have found an accusation against thee, and thou art worthy of death. For thou hast said that God himself should come down among the children of men; and now, for this cause thou shalt be put to death unless thou wilt recall all the words which thou hast spoken evil concerning me and my people."

Abinadi, who was not afraid of the king, replied, "I say unto you, I will not recall the words which I have spoken unto you concerning this people, for they are true; and that ye may know of their surety I have suffered myself that I have fallen into your hands. Yea, and I will suffer even until death, and I will not recall my words, and they shall stand as a testimony against you. And if ye slay me ye will shed innocent blood, and this shall also stand as a testimony against you at the last day."

The king, who was moved by what Abinadi said, would have released him, "for he feared that the judgments of God would come upon him." But the priests, seeing the king's determination weaken, began to accuse Abinadi, saying, "He has reviled the king." As a result, the angry king delivered Abinadi up to be slain.

"And it came to pass that they took him and bound him, and scourged his skin with faggots, yea, even unto death."

While the flames grew higher, Abinadi cried out one final message:

"Behold, even as ye have done unto me, so shall it come to pass that thy seed shall cause that many shall suffer the pains that I do suffer, even the pains of death by fire; and this because they believe in the salvation of the Lord their God.

"And it will come to pass that ye shall be afflicted with all manner of diseases because of your iniquities. Yea, and ye shall be smitten on every hand, and shall be driven and scattered to and fro, even as a wild flock is driven by wild and ferocious beasts. And in that day ye shall be hunted, and ye shall be taken by the hand of your enemies, and then ye shall suffer, as I suffer, the pains of death by fire.

"Thus God executeth vengeance upon those that destroy his people. O God, receive my soul."

Then Abinadi, having said these words, fell, "having suffered death by fire; yea, having been put to death because he would not deny the commandments of God, having sealed the truth of his words by his death." (Mosiah 17.)

Subsequently the Lamanites attacked the colony. King Noah fled with some of his priests and other attendants. He also ordered all the men of the city to flee, leaving their wives and children behind. Some obeyed, but many did not. Those who remained with their families went out to meet the Lamanites completely unarmed and pleaded for their lives. The hearts of the Lamanites were softened, and the people were spared. However, the Lamanites did enslave them and required them to pay a tribute of half of all their possessions and half of their crops and flocks.

The enslaved colonists chose as their king Limhi, a righteous son of Noah. Others in the city seem to have remained faithful also, because they gladly received Ammon and his company, who had been sent out from Zarahemla to find them. Ammon helped them to escape from the Lamanites and led them to Zarahemla.

Thus, all the prophecies of Abinadi were fulfilled, including the death of Noah, who was burned to death also.

Chapter 8

ALMA'S MINISTRY

Alma, the young priest who was converted by Abinadi's teachings, had been an evil man himself. The record says that he then "repented of his sins and iniquities, and went about privately among the people, and began to teach the words of Abinadi." (Mosiah 18:1.)

Later he told his followers about his former life of sin, saying, "Remember the iniquity of king Noah and his priests; and I myself was caught in a snare, and did many things which were abominable in the sight of the Lord, which caused me sore repentance. Nevertheless, after much tribulation, the Lord did hear my cries, and did answer my prayers, and has made me an instrument in his hands in bringing so many of you to a knowledge of his truth. Nevertheless, in this I do not glory, for I am unworthy to glory of myself." (Mosiah 23:9-10.)

The Lord instructed him by revelation and gave him divine authority to administer the ordinances of the gospel.

When the time came for the baptism of his followers, Alma officiated, "having authority from the Almighty God." (Mosiah 18:13.) The scripture says that those who were baptized were given the ordinance "by the power and authority of God." (Mosiah 18:17.)

The younger Alma was ordained by his father many years later. He reported that he had been consecrated by his father, Alma, "to be a high priest over the church of God, he having power and authority from God to do these things." (Alma 5:3.)

It becomes clear, then, that when Alma repented, the Lord fully accepted him and authorized him to be His servant in converting those who would follow him, and to baptize them for the remission of sins and admission into the church. No one need question his divine authority.

Alma went among the people in the city, quietly teaching the words of Abinadi. As is always the case in any community, there are righteous people even among the wicked. Some such persons were in Noah's kingdom also, and Alma found them. They, of course, had not heard Abinadi speak, for he delivered his message in the palace, where but few were allowed to come. Those who lived beyond the palace gates did not hear him. Some may have seen him as he was burned at the stake, however, for such events were public.

When Alma began to teach his friends the words of the martyred prophet, they responded gladly. He taught them "concerning the resurrection of the dead, and the redemption of the people, which was to be brought to pass through the power, and sufferings, and death of Christ, and his resurrection and ascension into heaven." The record says that "many did believe his words." (Mosiah 18:2-3.)

Alma made his headquarters in the wilderness near what was called the "waters of Mormon," a wooded area that provided privacy. His believers came to him there, and he taught them further of the gospel of Christ, details of which evidently were given him by revelation.

"As ye are desirous to come into the fold of God," he declared, "and to be called his people, and are willing to bear one another's burdens, that they may be light; yea, and are willing to mourn with those that mourn; yea, and comfort those that stand in need of comfort, and to stand as witnesses of God at all times and in all things, and in all places that ye may be in, even until death, that ye may be redeemed of God, and be numbered with those of the first resurrection, that ye may have eternal life—now I say unto you, if this be the desire of your hearts, what have you against being baptized in the name of the Lord, as a witness before him that ye have entered into a covenant with him, that ye will serve him and keep his commandments, that he may pour out his Spirit more abundantly upon you?"

When the people heard this, they "clapped their hands for joy, and exclaimed: This is the desire of our hearts."

The first person to be baptized was a man named Helam. His baptism is of particular interest, because when he was baptized, Alma immersed himself in the water also, since there was no one there authorized to baptize him. (Mosiah 18:8-14.)

This appears to be similar to what took place when Nephi began to baptize following the coming of the Savior after his resurrection. The scripture says that the twelve disciples "did pray for that which they most desired; and they desired that the Holy Ghost should be given unto them. And when they had thus prayed they went down unto the water's edge, and the multitude followed them.

"And it came to pass that Nephi went down into the water and was baptized. And he came up out of the water and began to baptize. And he baptized all those whom Jesus had chosen.

"And it came to pass when they were all baptized and had come up out of the water, the Holy Ghost did fall upon them, and they were filled with the Holy Ghost and with fire." (3 Nephi 19:9-13.)

Who baptized Nephi?

The record says concerning Alma:

"It came to pass that Alma took Helam, he being one of the first, and went and stood forth in the water, and cried, saying: O Lord, pour out thy Spirit upon thy servant, that he may do this work with holiness of heart.

"And when he had said these words, the Spirit of the Lord was upon him, and he said: Helam, I baptize thee, having authority from the Almighty God, as a testimony that ye have entered into a covenant to serve him until you are dead as to the mortal body; and may the Spirit of the Lord be poured out upon you; and may he grant unto you eternal life, through the redemption of Christ, whom he has prepared from the foundation of the world.

"And after Alma had said these words, both Alma and Helam were buried in the water; and they arose and came forth out of the water rejoicing, being filled with the Spirit.

"And again, Alma took another, and went forth a second time into the water, and baptized him according to the first, only he did not bury himself again in the water. And after this manner he did baptize every one that went forth to the place of Mormon; and they were in number about two hundred and four souls; yea, and they were baptized in the waters of Mormon, and were filled with the grace of God. And they were called the church of God, or the church of Christ, from that time forward. And it came to pass that whosoever was baptized by the power and authority of God was added to his church."

Alma ordained other men to the office of priest, and appointed one to each group of fifty people. He taught them that they should "preach nothing save it were repentance and faith on the Lord, who had redeemed his people."

Then Alma commanded the priests that "there should be no contention one with another, but that they should look forward with one eye, having one faith and one baptism, having their hearts knit together in unity and in love one towards another. And thus he commanded them to preach. And thus they became the children of God.

"And he commanded them that they should observe the sabbath day, and keep it holy, and also every day they should give thanks to the Lord their God. And he also commanded them that the priests whom he had ordained should labor with their own hands for their support. And there was one day in every week that was set apart that they should gather themselves together to teach the people, and to worship the Lord their God, and also, as often as it was in their power, to assemble themselves together."

Alma was particularly careful concerning the poor among them, for he commanded that "the people of the church should impart of their substance, every one according to that which he had; if he have more abundantly he should impart more abundantly; and of him that had but little, but little should be required; and to him that had not should be given. And thus they should impart of their substance of their own free will and good desires towards God, and to those priests that stood in need, yea, and to every needy, naked soul." (Mosiah 18:12-28.)

Chapter 9

ESCAPE FROM NOAH

King Noah, who was relentless in his search for Alma, set guards about the community, hoping that they would see him. Noticing a number of people moving toward the wilderness, the guards followed them to the waters of Mormon, where they had gathered together to hear the word of the Lord.

When King Noah was told this, he declared that Alma was "stirring up the people to rebellion against him," so he ordered his army sent out to destroy them.

"And it came to pass that Alma and the people of the Lord were apprised of the coming of the king's army; therefore they took their tents and their families and departed into the wilderness. And they were in number about four hundred and fifty souls." (Mosiah 18:32-35.)

Alma and his followers traveled for eight days into the wilderness and "came to a land, yea, even a very beautiful and pleasant land, a land of pure water." There they pitched their tents and began to till the soil. They also built permanent buildings so that they would not have to live in tents.

The people asked Alma to be their king and to rule over them. They had been accustomed to the reign of kings, since they had come out of Noah's kingdom over which Noah's father, Zeniff, had also reigned.

Alma was beloved by his people, the record says, but he was also wise. He told them, "It is not expedient that we should have a king; for thus saith the Lord: Ye shall not esteem one flesh above another, or one man shall not think himself above another; therefore I say unto you it is not expedient that ye should have a king. Nevertheless, if it were possible that ye could always have just men to be your kings it would be well for you to have a king."

Reminding them of the iniquity of King Noah and the manner in which he had led the people into degradation, Alma admitted that he himself had been caught in that snare, but now he had completely repented.

"Ye have been oppressed by king Noah," he said, "and have been in bondage to him and his priests, and have been brought into iniquity by them; therefore ye were bound with the bands of iniquity.

"And now as ye have been delivered by the power of God out of these bonds; yea, even out of the hands of king Noah and his people, and also from the bonds of iniquity, even so I desire that ye should stand fast in this liberty wherewith ye have been made free, and that ye trust no man to be a king over you. And also trust no one to be your teacher nor your minister, except he be a man of God, walking in his ways and keeping his commandments.

"Thus did Alma teach his people, that every man should love his neighbor as himself, that there should be no contention among them."

The Lord appointed Alma to be high priest over the people, and with this authority, Alma established the church of Jesus Christ among them.

"And it came to pass that none received authority to preach or to teach except it were by him from God. Therefore he consecrated all their priests and all their teachers; and none were consecrated except they were just men. Therefore they did watch over their people, and did nourish them with things pertaining to righteousness. And it came to pass that they began to prosper exceedingly in the land; and they called the land Helam."

Their peace did not continue, however, because suddenly and unexpectedly an army of the Lamanites approached them. The army had become lost on its way home after having been on an expedition, and the Nephites, who were out in their fields tending their crops and herds, were frightened. They fled to Alma in the city, and he assured them that the Lord would protect them.

"Therefore they hushed their fears, and began to cry unto the Lord that he would soften the hearts of the Lamanites, that they would spare them, and their wives, and their children. And it came to pass that the Lord did soften the hearts of the Lamanites. And Alma and his brethren went forth and delivered themselves up into their hands; and the Lamanites took possession of the land of Helam."

In its travels this army had found the wicked priests of King Noah who had escaped when Noah's city was invaded by the Lamanites and who had fled into the wilderness. When the Lamanite army found the priests, their leader, Amulon, pleaded with them. "He also sent forth their wives, who were the daughters of the Lamanites, to plead with their brethren, that they should not destroy their husbands. And the Lamanites had compassion on Amulon and his brethren, and did not destroy them, because of their wives."

As a result, Amulon and his brethren joined the Lamanites. The combined troops were traveling in the wilderness, searching for the land of Nephi, when they stumbled on the land of Helam.

The Lamanites promised Alma, as they approached his city, that if he would show them how to get back to the land of Nephi, they would not disturb his people, but in this they lied.

Amulon, who had by now been accepted by the Lamanites, recognized Alma as one of the former priests of King Noah. Ingratiating himself into the good graces of the Lamanites, he asked that he be made king of the land where Alma and his people lived. This request was granted, and immediately he began to oppress the people.

"And it came to pass that so great were their afflictions that they began to cry mightily to God. And Amulon commanded them that they should stop their cries; and he put guards over them to watch them, that whosoever should be found calling upon God should be put to death.

"And Alma and his people did not raise their voices to the Lord their God, but did pour out their hearts to him; and he did know the thoughts of their hearts."

As Alma and his people prayed mightily to the Lord for deliverance, the Lord responded and told them, "Lift up your heads and be of good comfort, for I know of the covenant which ye have made unto me; and I will covenant with my people and deliver them out of bondage. And I will also ease the burdens which are put upon your shoulders, that even you cannot feel them upon your backs, even while you are in bondage; and this will I do that ye may stand as witnesses for me hereafter, and that ye may know of a surety that I, the Lord God, do visit my people in their afflictions."

Then the Lord strengthened them "that they could bear up their burdens with ease," and they submitted "cheerfully and with patience to all the will of the Lord."

When the people exhibited great faith and patience, the Lord spoke again and said, "Be of good comfort, for on the morrow I will deliver you out of bondage."

Alma and his people spent the entire night preparing to leave their homes, gathering their flocks together and also packing up their grain. Then the Lord caused a deep sleep to come upon the Lamanites so that Alma and his people could leave in peace.

After traveling for twelve days, the people reached Zarahemla, where King Mosiah of the Nephites received them with joy. (Mosiah 24.)

After helping the people to become established in Zarahemla, King Mosiah gave Alma permission to establish branches of the church throughout Zarahemla. He also gave him "power to ordain priests and teachers over every church. Now this was done because there were so many people that they could not all be governed by one teacher; neither could they all hear the word of God in one assembly; therefore they did assemble themselves together in different bodies, being called churches; every church having their priests and their teachers, and every priest preaching the word according as it was delivered to him by the mouth of Alma.

"And thus, notwithstanding there being many churches they were all one church, yea, even the church of God; for there was nothing preached in all the churches except it were repentance and faith in God. And now there were seven churches in the land of Zarahemla. And it came to pass that whosoever were desirous to take upon them the name of Christ, or of God, they did join the churches of God; and they were called the people of God. And the Lord did pour out his Spirit upon them, and they were blessed, and prospered in the land." (Mosiah 25:20-24.)

Chapter 10

THE SAVIOR SPEAKS!

King Mosiah and Alma became close friends. Alma was now the head of the church, and Mosiah was head of the government. They worked closely together, and Mosiah protected the rights of the church and made laws against persecution.

A number of people in Zarahemla refused to believe the gospel.

"They did not believe what had been said concerning the resurrection of the dead, neither did they believe concerning the coming of Christ. And now because of their unbelief they could not understand the word of God; and their hearts were hardened. And they would not be baptized; neither would they join the church. And they were a separate people as to their faith, and remained so ever after, even in their carnal and sinful state; for they would not call upon the Lord their God."

The unbelievers were less than half as numerous as the members of the church, but because of the dissensions among the members, the skeptics became more numerous. This was a sad commentary. Because of the members' dissensions, the unbelievers prospered. It has ever been so. Apostasy breeds wickedness, and conflict among the members is always a comfort to the enemies of the church.

"It came to pass that they did deceive many with their flattering words, who were in the church, and did cause them to commit many sins; therefore it became expedient that those who committed sin, that were in the church, should be admonished by the church."

The teachers of the church brought the dissenting members before the priests, who took them to Alma hoping he, being the high priest, would judge them.

There had never been such a dissension among the people whom Alma had led, so he did not know how to handle the situation. He therefore went to the king for consultation, saying, "Here are many whom we have brought before thee, who are accused of their brethren, yea, and they have been taken in divers iniquities. And they do not repent of their iniquities, therefore we have brought them before thee, that thou mayest judge them according to their crimes."

Since it was a matter of apostasy within the church, and not an attack upon the government, the king put the matter back into Alma's hands.

That was no answer for Alma, who still did not know how to solve the problem, so he went to the Lord for direction. He received a direct revelation from Jesus Christ, the Savior. The Savior identified himself as "the Lord their God, . . . their Redeemer."

Speaking to Alma, the Lord said, "Blessed art thou, Alma, and blessed are they who were baptized in the waters of Mormon. Thou art blessed because of thy exceeding faith in the words alone of my servant Abinadi. And blessed are they because of their exceeding faith in the words alone which thou hast spoken unto them. And blessed art thou because thou hast established a church among this people; and they shall be established, and they shall be my people. Yea, blessed is this people who are willing to bear my name; for in my name shall they be called; and they are mine."

The Lord referred directly to Alma's request for direction about the apostates, saying, "Because thou hast inquired of me concerning the transgressor, thou art blessed. Thou art my servant; and I covenant with thee that thou shalt have eternal life; and thou shalt serve me and go forth in my name, and shalt gather together my sheep."

Then the Lord declared, "He that will hear my voice shall be my sheep; and him shall ye receive into the church, and him will I also receive. For behold, this is my church; whosoever is baptized shall be baptized unto repentance. And whomsoever ye receive shall believe in my name; and him will I freely forgive. For it is I that taketh upon me the sins of the world; for it is I that hath created them; and it is I that granteth unto him that believeth unto the end a place at my right hand."

Note here that the Savior declared himself to be the Creator: "It is I that hath created them." He went on to say that if those who are called in his name know him, they shall come forth and shall have a place eternally at his right hand.

Then the Lord continued in this remarkable revelation to Alma:

"It shall come to pass that when the second trump shall sound then shall they that never knew me come forth and shall stand before me. And then shall they know that I am the Lord their God, that I am their Redeemer; but they would not be redeemed. And then I will confess unto them that I never knew them; and they shall depart into everlasting fire prepared for the devil and his angels.

"Therefore I say unto you, that he that will not hear my voice, the same shall ye not receive into my church, for him I will not receive at the last day.

"Therefore I say unto you, Go; and whosoever transgresseth against me, him shall ye judge according to the sins which he has committed; and if he confess his sins before thee and me, and repenteth in the sincerity of his heart, him shall ye forgive, and I will forgive him also.

"Yea, and as often as my people repent will I forgive them their trespasses against me. And ye shall also forgive one another your trespasses; for verily I say unto you, he that forgiveth not his neighbor's trespasses when he says that he repents, the same hath brought himself unto condemnation.

"Now I say unto you, Go; and whosoever will not repent of his sins the same shall not be numbered among my people; and this shall be observed from this time forward."

Alma recorded this revelation for use in his ministry whenever he had to judge wicked members of the church.

"And it came to pass that Alma went and judged those that

had been taken in iniquity, according to the word of the Lord. And whosoever repented of their sins and did confess them, them he did number among the people of the church; and those that would not confess their sins and repent of their iniquity, the same were not numbered among the people of the church, and their names were blotted out.

"And it came to pass that Alma did regulate all the affairs of the church; and they began again to have peace and to prosper exceedingly in the affairs of the church, walking circumspectly before God, receiving many, and baptizing many." (Mosiah 26.)

Chapter 11

ALMA THE YOUNGER

Among the apostates who began to fight against the church were Alma's own son, whom he had named after himself, and the sons of King Mosiah.

Mosiah's sons were a great embarrassment, as was Alma the younger. The record says that young Alma "became a very wicked and idolatrous man. And he was a man of many words and did speak much flattery to the people. Therefore he led many of the people to do after the manner of his iniquities.

"And he became a great hinderment to the prosperity of the church of God; stealing away the hearts of the people; causing much dissension among the people; giving a chance for the enemy of God to exercise his power over them." (Mosiah 27:9.)

Alma and the sons of Mosiah went about the church destroying faith wherever they went, "seeking to destroy the church, and to lead astray the people of the Lord, contrary to the commandments of God, or even the king." (Mosiah 27:10.)

Of the sons of Mosiah the record says, "They were the very vilest of sinners." (Mosiah 28:4.) These young men were named Ammon, Aaron, Omner, and Himni. But like Saul of Tarsus, they were "chosen vessels of the Lord," and their great talents were needed in the church. And, like Saul of Tarsus, they were stopped in their wickedness by a heavenly manifestation:

"As they were going about rebelling against God, behold, the angel of the Lord appeared unto them; and he descended as it were in a cloud; and he spake as it were with a voice of thunder, which caused the earth to shake upon which they stood; and so great was their astonishment, that they fell to the earth, and understood not the words which he spake unto them.

"Nevertheless he cried again, saying: Alma, arise and stand forth, for why persecutest thou the church of God? For the Lord hath said: This is my church, and I will establish it; and nothing shall overthrow it, save it is the transgression of my people.

"And again, the angel said: Behold, the Lord hath heard the prayers of his people, and also the prayers of his servant, Alma, who is thy father; for he has prayed with much faith concerning thee that thou mightest be brought to the knowledge of the truth; therefore, for this purpose have I come to convince thee of the power and authority of God, that the prayers of his servants might be answered according to their faith.

"And now behold, can ye dispute the power of God? For behold, doth not my voice shake the earth? And can ye not also behold me before you? And I am sent from God.

"Now I say unto thee: Go, and remember the captivity of thy fathers in the land of Helam, and in the land of Nephi; and remember how great things he has done for them; for they were in bondage, and he has delivered them. And now I say unto thee, Alma, go thy way, and seek to destroy the church no more, that their prayers may be answered, and this even if thou wilt of thyself be cast off."

The young men fell to the earth with astonishment, "for with their own eyes they had beheld an angel of the Lord; and his voice was as thunder, which shook the earth; and they knew that there was nothing save the power of God that could shake the earth and cause it to tremble as though it would part asunder."

Alma the younger was struck dumb, and his strength ebbed away. He was so weak that he could not walk, and being dumb, he could not speak.

Mosiah's sons, not so afflicted, carried young Alma to the home of his father and laid him down, helpless, before him. They explained all that had happened, and the father rejoiced, "for he knew that it was the power of God."

Alma called the people in the area to come and see his son

and to learn what had happened. He then called a number of the priests of the church to come and fast and pray that the youth might regain both his speech and his physical strength. This the father did "that the eyes of the people might be opened to see and know of the goodness and glory of God."

For two days and nights the priests fasted and prayed, and then Alma the younger received his strength. He stood up before all of the people and began to speak to them. It was a great miracle, but even greater was the transformation that had taken place within. This young man, formerly so sinful and rebellious, had been given a change of heart by the Lord. As he stood before the people, and his own father, he said:

"I have repented of my sins, and have been redeemed of the Lord; behold I am born of the Spirit.

"And the Lord said unto me: Marvel not that all mankind, yea, men and women, all nations, kindreds, tongues and people, must be born again; yea, born of God, changed from their carnal and fallen state, to a state of righteousness, being redeemed of God, becoming his sons and daughters. And thus they become new creatures; and unless they do this, they can in nowise inherit the kingdom of God.

"I say unto you, unless this be the case, they must be cast off; and this I know, because I was like to be cast off. Nevertheless, after wandering through much tribulation, repenting nigh unto death, the Lord in mercy hath seen fit to snatch me out of an everlasting burning, and I am born of God.

"My soul hath been redeemed from the gall of bitterness and bonds of iniquity. I was in the darkest abyss; but now I behold the marvelous light of God. My soul was racked with eternal torment; but I am snatched, and my soul is pained no more.

"I rejected my Redeemer, and denied that which had been spoken of by our fathers; but now that they may foresee that he will come, and that he remembereth every creature of his creating, he will make himself manifest unto all. Yea, every knee shall bow, and every tongue confess before him. Yea, even at the last day, when all men shall stand to be judged of him, then shall they confess that he is God; then shall they confess, who live without God in the world, that the judgment of an everlasting punishment is just upon them; and they shall quake, and tremble, and shrink beneath the glance of his all-searching eye."

The sons of Mosiah were similarly reborn, and the group again began visiting the church, this time to repair the damage they had done and to declare their repentance and conversion as a result of the visitation of the angel.

Their former friends, the apostates, turned against them and bitterly persecuted them, but they continued on, "zealously striving to repair all the injuries which they had done to the church, confessing all their sins, and publishing all the things which they had seen, and explaining the prophecies and the scriptures to all who desired to hear them.

"And thus they were instruments in the hands of God in bringing many to the knowledge of the truth, yea, to the knowledge of their Redeemer. And how blessed are they! For they did publish peace; they did publish good tidings of good; and they did declare unto the people that the Lord reigneth." (Mosiah 27:11-37.)

Chapter 12

THE TRANSFORMATION

Great changes now came to the Nephites.

King Mosiah was growing old, and so was Alma. The king desired to bestow the crown upon one of his sons, but all four of them rejected the idea. Now that they had been converted to Christ, their whole desire was to preach his word. Thus, they went to King Mosiah and asked permission to leave Zarahemla and go over into the land of Nephi to preach the gospel to the Lamanites. They sincerely desired to bring the word of God to those people in the hope of reforming them, bringing them salvation, and to preserve peace in the land.

Their father, a prophet as well as a king, inquired of the Lord. He responded, saying, "Let them go up, for many shall believe on their words, and they shall have eternal life; and I will deliver thy sons out of the hands of the Lamanites." (Mosiah 28:7.)

With this instruction, Mosiah permitted his sons to leave.

The younger Alma devoted himself to the ministry in Zarahemla and worked closely with his own father, who was high priest over the church in all the land. He progressed rapidly in the work of the Lord and was completely devoted in every way.

With the father growing old—he was now past eighty years of age—Alma the younger steadily took over more and more of the ministry; subsequently, he became high priest in the place of his father.

With no son on whom to bestow the crown, Mosiah now decided that there should not be a king to succeed him, but that there should be a government of the people and by the people.

He sent a proclamation out to all the land in which he announced that he would continue to reign as long as he lived, but that the people should now prepare to rule themselves through men whom they would choose "by the voice of the people."

He spoke of the evil caused by unrighteous kings: "How much iniquity doth one wicked king cause to be committed, yea, and what great destruction! . . . The sins of many people have been caused by the iniquities of their kings; therefore their iniquities are answered upon the heads of their kings." (Mosiah 29:17, 31.)

Emphasizing the importance of this fact, Mosiah said, "Yea, remember king Noah, his wickedness and his abominations, and also the wickedness and abominations of his people. Behold what great destruction did come upon them; and also because of their iniquities they were brought into bondage. . . .

"Now I say unto you, ye cannot dethrone an iniquitous king save it be through much contention, and the shedding of much blood. For behold, he has his friends in iniquity, and he keepeth his guards about him; and he teareth up the laws of those who have reigned in righteousness before him; and he trampleth under his feet the commandments of God." (Mosiah 29:18, 21-22.)

King Mosiah then laid down the principles of free government by which the Nephites were to govern themselves:

"Therefore, choose you by the voice of this people, judges, that ye may be judged according to the laws which have been given you by our fathers, which are correct, and which were given them by the hand of the Lord.

"Now it is not common that the voice of the people desireth anything contrary to that which is right; but it is common for the lesser part of the people to desire that which is not right; therefore this shall ye observe and make it your law—to do your business by the voice of the people.

"And if the time comes that the voice of the people doth

choose iniquity, then is the time that the judgments of God will come upon you; yea, then is the time he will visit you with great destruction even as he has hitherto visited this land." (Mosiah 29:25-27.)

King Mosiah was willing to give up his own throne and divest his family of all the privileges of royalty in order to set up a free government in this hemisphere. But he knew that even with democratic rule, God must be a part of it or it would fail. So he said, "I command you to do these things in the fear of the Lord; and I command you to do these things, and that ye have no king; that if these people commit sins and iniquities they shall be answered upon their own heads." (Mosiah 29:30.)

When the Lord gave to modern America its free form of government, he had the same thing in mind. He said that the laws and the Constitution of the United States should be "maintained for the rights and protection of all flesh, according to just and holy principles; that every man may act in doctrine and principle pertaining to futurity according to the moral agency which I have given unto him, that every man may be accountable for his own sins in the day of judgment.

"Therefore, it is not right that any man should be in bondage one to another. And for this purpose have I established the Constitution of this land, by the hands of wise men whom I raised up unto this very purpose, and redeemed the land by the shedding of blood." (D&C 101:77-80.)

Further, the Lord said through the Prophet Joseph Smith, "I, the Lord God, make you free, therefore ye are free indeed; and the law also maketh you free." (D&C 98:8.)

Freedom of choice was first given to man in the Garden of Eden, when the Lord told Adam that he could choose for himself. There is no eternal advancement without it.

It is notable that in both the case of Mosiah and the Constitution of the United States, God's rules of righteousness were intended to be part and parcel of the government. Mosiah said that the judges to be elected were to administer the laws that were given by their fathers, "which are correct, and which were given them by the hand of the Lord." (Mosiah 29:25.)

With respect to the Constitution of the United States the Lord said it "should be maintained for the rights and protection of all flesh, according to just and holy principles." (D&C 101:77.) Thus we see that a government by the voice of the people was established in America a century before the birth of Christ.

Alma the younger "was appointed to be the first chief judge, he being also the high priest, his father having conferred the office upon him, and having given him the charge concerning all the affairs of the church.

"And now it came to pass that Alma did walk in the ways of the Lord, and he did keep his commandments, and he did judge righteous judgments; and there was continual peace through the land. And thus commenced the reign of the judges throughout all the land of Zarahemla, among all the people who were called the Nephites; and Alma was the first and chief judge." (Mosiah 29:42-44.)

King Mosiah had been a prophet as well as a king to his people, and God recognized him as such. The Lord had committed to his care the many sacred records compiled through the years. He also possessed the Urim and Thummim by which he could read ancient languages, and when the Jaredite plates were brought to him, he was able to translate them. They became what we know as the book of Ether.

Failing in health, Mosiah felt that his end was near, and so he "took the plates of brass, and all things which he had kept, and conferred them upon Alma, who was the son of Alma; yea, all the records, and also the interpreters, and conferred them upon him, and commanded him that he should keep and preserve them, and also keep a record of the people, handing them down from one generation to another, even as they had been handed down from the time that Lehi left Jerusalem." (Mosiah 28:20.)

The elder Alma passed away at age eighty-two. "And it came to pass that Mosiah died also, in the thirty and third year of his reign, being sixty and three years old; making in the whole, five hundred and nine years from the time Lehi left Jerusalem. And thus ended the reign of the kings over the people of Nephi; and thus ended the days of Alma, who was the founder of their church." (Mosiah 29:46-47.)

Chapter 13

THE LAWS OF JUSTICE

When Mosiah prescribed a government "by the voice of the people," he decreed that the laws to be used should be those handed down from the fathers that had been given to them by the Lord. We do not know what all of those laws were, but we do know that the Ten Commandments were among them, because Abinadi made such a point of them in his discussion with the priests of Noah. Obviously there were many others. Among those mentioned in the scriptures were:

1. *Capital punishment for murder.* This is indicated in many parts of the Book of Mormon. The Nephites had the Old Testament on the brass plates, which were handed down with the plates they themselves had made. In Genesis it was specifically decreed that "whoso sheddeth man's blood, by man shall his blood be shed." (Genesis 9:6.)

The Nephites had their own locally made laws as well. When the wicked Nehor killed Gideon he was sentenced to death. The record says:

"And thou hast shed the blood of a righteous man, yea, a man who has done much good among this people; and were we to spare thee his blood would come upon us for vengeance. Therefore thou art condemned to die, according to the law which has been given us by Mosiah, our last king; and it has been acknowledged by this people; therefore this people must abide by the law.

"And it came to pass that they took him; and his name was Nehor; and they carried him upon the top of the hill Manti, and there he was caused, or rather did acknowledge, between the heavens and the earth, that what he had taught to the people was contrary to the word of God; and there he suffered an ignominious death." (Alma 1:13-15.)

In 2 Nephi 9:35 we read that the murderer who deliberately kills shall die. In Alma we read, "If he murdered he was punished unto death" (Alma 30:10), and "The law requireth the life of him who hath murdered" (Alma 34:12).

2. *Other crimes,* as listed in the Ten Commandments, included adultery, stealing, and lying. There was punishment provided for all such violations.

"They durst not lie, if it were known, for fear of the law, for liars were punished; therefore they pretended to preach according to their belief; and now the law could have no power on any man for his belief. And they durst not steal, for fear of the law, for such were punished; neither durst they rob, nor murder, for he that murdered was punished unto death." (Alma 1:17-18.)

3. *Slavery* was specifically prohibited. "It is against the law of our brethren . . . that there should be any slaves among them." (Alma 27:9.)

4. *Strife* was legislated against, including rioting and mobocracy. "Now those priests who did go forth among the people did preach against all lyings, strifes, and malice, and revilings, and stealing, robbing, plundering, murdering, . . . crying that these things ought not so to be." (Alma 16:18.)

Persecution, in the sense of physical abuse, was forbidden, although there were instances when name-calling and mental harassment went unpunished.

"Now there was a strict law among the people of the church, that there should not any man, belonging to the church, arise and persecute those that did not belong to the church, and that there should be no persecution among themselves." (Alma 1:21.)

5. *Freedom of religion* was protected by law.

"There was no law against a man's belief; for it was strictly contrary to the commands of God that there should be a law which should bring men on to unequal grounds.

"For thus saith the scripture: Choose ye this day, whom ye will serve. Now if a man desired to serve God, it was his privilege; or rather, if he believed in God it was his privilege to serve him; but if he did not believe in him there was no law to punish him.

"But if he murdered he was punished unto death; and if he robbed he was also punished; and if he stole he was also punished; and if he committed adultery he was also punished; yea, for all this wickedness they were punished." (Alma 30: 7-10.)

6. *Punishments* were meted out according to the gravity of the crime.

"For there was a law that men should be judged according to their crimes. Nevertheless, there was no law against a man's belief; therefore, a man was punished only for the crimes which he had done; therefore all men were on equal grounds." (Alma 30:11.)

The Nephites were taught the gospel of Christ, and the Lord communicated with their prophets. But the Nephites were also required to continue living under the law of Moses, for it had not yet been fulfilled. The Savior himself would accomplish that through his atonement. Much of the government of the Nephites might be called a theocracy. There were judges for the civil laws, but priests for the law of Moses. Though at times the Nephites had kings who made civil laws, they still were under the law of Moses. With the righteous kings, the civil law harmonized completely with the law of Moses insofar as conduct and punishments were concerned.

In Old Testament times in Palestine such severe crimes as adultery were punished by death. There is no evidence in the Book of Mormon that adulterers were stoned to death in America as was the case in Palestine.

As Abinadi had pointed out, "it was expedient that there should be a law given to the children of Israel, yea, even a very strict law, for they were a stiff-necked people, and slow to remember the Lord their God. Therefore, there was a law given them, yea, a law of performances and of ordinances, a law which they were to observe strictly from day to day, to keep them in remembrance of God and their duty towards him. But behold, I say unto you, that all these things were types of things to come.

"And now, did they understand the law? I say unto you, Nay, they did not all understand the law; and this because of the hardness of their hearts; for they understood not that there could not any man be saved except it were through the redemption of God." (Mosiah 13:30-32.)

As the Nephite records show, the rule of judges chosen by the voice of the people was generally effective, although there were crises from time to time, as in the time of the great Captain Moroni when "kingmen" arose, seeking to overthrow the rule of the people and reestablish the monarchy. Much blood was shed over that, but men like Moroni and Pahoran preserved peace by law, despite all the efforts of the "kingmen."

Wicked rulers such as King Noah discarded the laws of God and the righteous laws of men. They set up their own wicked rules to justify all their immoralities, dishonest practices, concubines, robberies, and idolatries.

In the two hundred years following the visitation of the Savior, the law was that of the gospel.

"And it came to pass that there was no contention in the land, because of the love of God which did dwell in the hearts of the people.

"And there were no envyings, nor strifes, nor tumults, nor whoredoms, nor lyings, nor murders, nor any manner of lasciviousness; and surely there could not be a happier people among all the people who had been created by the hand of God.

"There were no robbers, nor murderers, neither were there Lamanites, nor any manner of -ites; but they were in one, the children of Christ, and heirs to the kingdom of God.

"And how blessed were they! For the Lord did bless them

in all their doings; yea, even they were blessed and prospered until an hundred and ten years had passed away; and the first generation from Christ had passed away, and there was no contention in all the land." (4 Nephi 1:15-18.)

This was the golden age of all time—anywhere—and it lasted as long as people were willing to live the gospel of Christ. When they departed from His law, however, selfishness arose, crime developed, and eventually mighty wars wiped out the Nephites entirely.

Chapter 14

THE CHURCH ORGANIZED

In the Nephite record, repeated references are made to the establishment of the church from time to time, either in new cities or following apostasies in the older ones. There is no clear description of its form of organization, however. Early in his work, soon after he left Noah's influence, Alma ordained teachers and priests and set them over congregations of fifty people each.

Reference is made later to the ordination of elders. Alma consecrated elders "over the church" (Alma 6:1) and he gave one of them "power to enact laws" (Alma 4:16).

The scripture specifically says that Alma was a high priest in the high priesthood after the order of the Son of God. (Alma 13:1-11.) Ammon was a high priest over the Ammonites (Alma 30:20), and Helaman and his brethren became high priests over the church (Alma 46:6).

Alma talked freely about this higher priesthood "after the order of his [God's] Son," which we today know as the Melchizedek Priesthood.

We are told in the Doctrine and Covenants that "there are, in the church, two priesthoods, namely, the Melchizedek and Aaronic, including the Levitical Priesthood.

"Why the first is called the Melchizedek Priesthood is because Melchizedek was such a great high priest. Before his day it was called *the Holy Priesthood, after the Order of the Son of God*. But out of respect or reverence to the name of the Supreme Being, to avoid the too frequent repetition of his name, they, the church, in ancient days, called that priesthood after Melchizedek, or the Melchizedek Priesthood." (D&C 107:1-4.)

When Alma discussed this higher priesthood he said:

"Or in fine, in the first place they were on the same standing with their brethren; thus this holy calling being prepared from the foundation of the world for such as would not harden their hearts, being in and through the atonement of the Only Begotten Son, who was prepared—

"And thus being called by this holy calling, and ordained unto the high priesthood of the holy order of God, to teach his commandments unto the children of men, that they also might enter into his rest—

"This high priesthood being after the order of his Son, which order was from the foundation of the world; or in other words, being without beginning of days or end of years, being prepared from eternity to all eternity, according to his foreknowledge of all things—

"Now they were ordained after this manner—being called with a holy calling, and ordained with a holy ordinance, and taking upon them the high priesthood of the holy order, which calling, and ordinance, and high priesthood, is without beginning or end—

"Thus they become high priests forever, after the order of the Son, the Only Begotten of the Father, who is without beginning of days or end of years, who is full of grace, equity, and truth. And thus it is. Amen.

"Now, as I said concerning the holy order of this high priesthood, there were many who were ordained and became high priests of God; and it was on account of their exceeding faith and repentance, and their righteousness before God, they choosing to repent and work righteousness rather than to perish;

"Therefore they were called after this holy order, and were sanctified, and their garments were washed white through the blood of the Lamb."

Alma was familiar with the place of Melchizedek in the church of God. He said:

"And now, my brethren, I would that ye should humble

yourselves before God, and bring forth fruit meet for repentance, that ye may also enter into that rest.

"Yea, humble yourselves even as the people in the days of Melchizedek, who was also a high priest after this same order which I have spoken, who also took upon him the high priesthood forever. And it was this same Melchizedek to whom Abraham paid tithes; yea, even our father Abraham paid tithes of one-tenth part of all he possessed.

"Now these ordinances were given after this manner, that thereby the people might look forward on the Son of God, it being a type of his order, or it being his order, and this that they might look forward to him for a remission of their sins, that they might enter into the rest of the Lord.

"Now this Melchizedek was a king over the land of Salem; and his people had waxed strong in iniquity and abomination; yea, they had all gone astray; they were full of all manner of wickedness; but Melchizedek having exercised mighty faith, and received the office of the high priesthood according to the holy order of God, did preach repentance unto his people. And behold, they did repent; and Melchizedek did establish peace in the land in his days; therefore he was called the prince of peace, for he was the king of Salem; and he did reign under his father.

"Now, there were many before him, and also there were many afterwards, but none were greater; therefore, of him they have more particularly made mention."

The scriptures available to the people of Alma's day evidently had full information on this subject, for Alma said, "Now I need not rehearse the matter; what I have said may suffice. Behold, the scriptures are before you; if ye will wrest them it shall be to your own destruction." (Alma 13:5-20.)

The Nephites had temples over a period of centuries. We do not know what the ordinances consisted of. There was no work for the dead, because that was reserved until after the crucifixion and resurrection of the Lord.

But there were many temples, some in the time of the first

Nephi (2 Nephi 5:16); at least one temple in the land Bountiful at the time of Christ (3 Nephi 11:1); a temple in the time of Mosiah (Mosiah 1:18); and a temple in Zeniff's kingdom, which was still standing in the time of the wicked King Noah, who added frills to it (Mosiah 11:10, 12). Noah's kingdom was but a small colony separated from the main body of Nephites.

An indication that there were many temples is seen in the comments of Mormon as he wrote the Book of Helaman. When he spoke of people going into the land northward he said, "And the people who were in the land northward did dwell in tents, and in houses of cement, and they did suffer whatsoever tree should spring up upon the face of the land that it should grow up, that in time they might have timber to build their houses, yea, their cities, and their temples, and their synagogues, and their sanctuaries, and all manner of their buildings." (Helaman 3:9.)

And when he expanded on his account of this migration, he spoke of "their preaching and their prophecies, and their shipping and their building of ships, and their building of temples, and of synagogues and their sanctuaries." (Helaman 3:14.)

What ordinances were performed in those temples and by what priesthood authority is not indicated, but since the people lived under the law of Moses as well as the gospel of Christ, and since their ancestors had known the temple in Jerusalem, there can be little doubt about their activity in temple work.

Chapter 15

PERSECUTIONS ARISE

From the beginning of Alma's reign as chief judge, conflicts arose among the people, chiefly due to opposition from the non-believers. Many loved the "vain things of the world, and they went forth preaching false doctrines; and this they did for the sake of riches and honor. . . .

"But it came to pass that whosoever did not belong to the church of God began to persecute those that did belong to the church of God, and had taken upon them the name of Christ.

"Yea, they did persecute them, and afflict them with all manner of words, and this because of their humility; because they were not proud in their own eyes, and because they did impart the word of God, one with another, without money and without price.

"Now there was a strict law among the people of the church that there should not any man, belonging to the church, arise and persecute those that did not belong to the church, and that there should be no persecution among themselves.

"Nevertheless, there were many among them who began to be proud, and began to contend warmly with their adversaries, even unto blows; yea, they would smite one another with their fists."

Among the faithful members of the Church there was great sincerity of worship. They had no paid clergy, and all labored for their own living. "And when the priests left their labor to impart the word of God unto the people, the people also left their labors to hear the word of God. And when the priest had imparted unto them the word of God they all returned again diligently unto their labors; and the priest, not esteeming himself above his hearers, for the preacher was no better than the hearer, neither was the teacher any better than the learner; and thus they were all equal, and they did all labor, every man according to his strength." The priests were mindful of the poor; they did not wear costly apparel, "yet they were neat and comely."

The members began to prosper abundantly, but still "they did not send away any who were naked, or that were hungry, or that were athirst, or that were sick, or that had not been nourished; and they did not set their hearts upon riches; therefore they were liberal to all, both old and young, both bond and free, both male and female, whether out of the church or in the church, having no respect to persons as to those who stood in need.

"And thus they did prosper and become far more wealthy than those who did not belong to their church."

Those who did not belong to the church indulged "in sorceries, and in idolatry or idleness, and in babblings, and in envyings and strife; wearing costly apparel; being lifted up in the pride of their own eyes; lying, thieving, robbing, committing whoredoms, and murdering, and all manner of wickedness; nevertheless, the law was put in force upon all those who did transgress it, inasmuch as it was possible."

Through a strict enforcement of the law, persecution was largely discontinued, and peace prevailed for the first five years of the reign of the judges. (Alma 1.)

Chapter 16

AMLICI'S REBELLION

Dissension arose in the fifth year of the reign of the judges, caused by a crafty man named Amlici, who attempted to set himself up as a king, thus destroying the free government under which the people lived. Through his persuasion, he gained numerous followers. This caused many disputations among the people, and it was arranged that assemblies be held in which advocates of Amlici's kingship could debate the issue with the people who favored freedom.

The scripture says that every man could speak according to his own mind, "whether it were for or against Amlici . . . having much dispute and wonderful contentions one with another. And thus they did assemble themselves together to cast in their voices concerning the matter," and their arguments were laid before the judges of the land.

Those who were against Amlici, being in the majority, were grateful that the voice of the people could be expressed and that the decisions would be made through the system of judges.

But this did not please Amlici. He refused to abide by the free choice of the people. His followers grouped together and consecrated Amlici to be king over the land. He armed his followers and immediately ordered them to begin a war against the rest of the people.

"Alma, being the chief judge and the governor of the people of Nephi, therefore he went up with his people, yea, with his captains, and chief captains, yea, at the head of his armies, against the Amlicites to battle. And they began to slay the Amlicites upon the hill east of Sidon. And the Amlicites did contend with the Nephites with great strength, insomuch that many of the Nephites did fall before the Amlicites.

"Nevertheless the Lord did strengthen the hand of the Nephites, that they slew the Amlicites with great slaughter, that they began to flee before them.

"And it came to pass that the Nephites did pursue the Amlicites all that day, and did slay them with much slaughter, insomuch that there were slain of the Amlicites twelve thousand five hundred thirty and two souls; and there were slain of the Nephites six thousand five hundred sixty and two souls."

Alma's men pursued the Amlicites for a time, and then sent out spies to watch their camps. To their great astonishment, an army of Lamanites came, joined the Amlicites, and renewed the attack.

"Nevertheless, the Nephites being strengthened by the hand of the Lord, having prayed mightily to him that he would deliver them out of the hands of their enemies, therefore the Lord did hear their cries, and did strengthen them, and the Lamanites and the Amlicites did fall before them.

"And it came to pass that Alma fought with Amlici with the sword, face to face; and they did contend mightily, one with another. And it came to pass that Alma, being a man of God, being exercised with much faith, cried, saying: O Lord, have mercy and spare my life, that I may be an instrument in thy hands to save and preserve this people.

"Now when Alma had said these words he contended again with Amlici; and he was strengthened, insomuch that he slew Amlici with the sword. And he also contended with the king of the Lamanites; but the king of the Lamanites fled back from before Alma and sent his guards to contend with Alma. But Alma, with his guards, contended with the guards of the king of the Lamanites until he slew and drove them back." (Alma 2.)

The Nephites drove their enemies completely out of their land. It was a great victory, for which they thanked the Lord, acknowledging that they had fought with the strength of God.

Alma now saw the importance of spending more time in the ministry, and he felt that he must assign the office of chief judge to someone else. He found a humble and faithful man named Nephihah "and gave him power according to the voice of the people, that he might have power to enact laws according to the laws which had been given, and to put them in force according to the wickedness and the crimes of the people." (Alma 4:16.)

Alma retained the office of high priest and gave only the judgment seat to Nephihah. "And this he did that he himself might go forth among his people, or among the people of Nephi, that he might preach the word of God unto them, to stir them up in remembrance of their duty, and that he might pull down, by the word of God, all the pride and craftiness and all the contentions which were among his people, seeing no way that he might reclaim them save it were in bearing down in pure testimony against them." (Alma 4:19.)

Chapter 17

THE BREAD
OF LIFE

Alma undertook a missionary journey among all the cities of the Nephites. Grieved at the sin that existed everywhere, he determined to make a nationwide call for repentance. He began in Zarahemla and then went from city to city, preaching Christ and the Atonement and appealing for strict obedience to the commandments.

Telling the people of the conversion of his father and of his own conversion as well, he stressed the importance of a changed heart and an obedient spirit:

"Can ye imagine yourselves brought before the tribunal of God with your souls filled with guilt and remorse, having a remembrance of all your guilt, yea, a perfect remembrance of all your wickedness, yea, a remembrance that ye have set at defiance the commandments of God?

"I say unto you, can ye look up to God at that day with a pure heart and clean hands? I say unto you, can you look up, having the image of God engraven upon your countenances? I say unto you, can ye think of being saved when you have yielded yourselves to become subjects to the devil?

"I say unto you, ye will know at that day that ye cannot be saved; for there can no man be saved except his garments are washed white; yea, his garments must be purified until they are cleansed from all stain, through the blood of him of whom it has been spoken by our fathers, who should come to redeem his people from their sins.

"And now I ask of you, my brethren, how will any of you feel, if ye shall stand before the bar of God, having your garments stained with blood and all manner of filthiness? Behold, what will these things testify against you? Behold will they not testify that ye are murderers, yea, and also that ye are guilty of all manner of wickedness?" (Alma 5:18-23.)

Alma was forceful and he was direct. Soft speech would not accomplish his purpose. He continued as he spoke of Christ:

"Behold, I say unto you, that the good shepherd doth call you; yea, and in his own name he doth call you, which is the name of Christ; and if ye will not hearken unto the voice of the good shepherd, to the name by which ye are called, behold, ye are not the sheep of the good shepherd. And now if ye are not the sheep of the good shepherd, of what fold are ye? Behold, I say unto you, that the devil is your shepherd, and ye are of his fold; and now, who can deny this? Behold, I say unto you, whosoever denieth this is a liar and a child of the devil. For I say unto you that whatsoever is good cometh from God, and whatsoever is evil cometh from the devil." (Alma 5:38-40.)

Asserting his right to preach, Alma declared:

"For I am called to speak after this manner, according to the holy order of God, which is in Christ Jesus; yea, I am commanded to stand and testify unto this people the things which have been spoken by our fathers concerning the things which are to come.

"And this is not all. Do ye not suppose that I know of these things myself? Behold, I testify unto you that I do know that these things whereof I have spoken are true. And how do ye suppose that I know of their surety? Behold, I say unto you they are made known unto me by the Holy Spirit of God. Behold, I have fasted and prayed many days that I might know these things of myself. And now I do know of myself that they are true; for the Lord God hath made them manifest unto me by his Holy Spirit; and this is the spirit of revelation which is in me."

Alma then bore a mighty testimony of the Savior:

"I say unto you, that I know of myself that whatsoever I shall say unto you, concerning that which is to come, is true; and I say unto you, that I know that Jesus Christ shall come, yea, the Son, the Only Begotten of the Father, full of grace, and mercy, and truth. And behold, it is he that cometh to take away the sins of the world, yea, the sins of every man who steadfastly believeth on his name.

"And now I say unto you that this is the order after which I am called, yea, to preach unto my beloved brethren, yea, and every one that dwelleth in the land; yea, to preach unto all, both old and young, both bond and free; yea, I say unto you the aged, and also the middle aged, and the rising generation; yea, to cry unto them that they must repent and be born again.

"Yea, thus saith the Spirit: Repent, all ye ends of the earth, for the kingdom of heaven is soon at hand; yea, the Son of God cometh in his glory, in his might, majesty, power, and dominion. Yea, my beloved brethren, I say unto you, that the Spirit saith: Behold the glory of the King of all the earth; and also the King of heaven shall very soon shine forth among all the children of men." (Alma 5:38-50.)

This was Alma's appeal to the people of the city of Zarahemla. In preparation for a favorable response, he ordained more priests and elders by the laying on of hands "according to the order of God" to preside and watch over the church. Then he went to the city of Gideon, where again he preached Christ:

"But behold, the Spirit hath said this much unto me, saying: Cry unto this people, saying—Repent ye, and prepare the way of the Lord, and walk in his paths, which are straight; for behold, the kingdom of heaven is at hand, and the Son of God cometh upon the face of the earth.

"And behold, he shall be born of Mary, at Jerusalem which is the land of our forefathers, she being a virgin, a precious and chosen vessel, who shall be overshadowed and conceive by the power of the Holy Ghost, and bring forth a son, yea, even the Son of God.

"And he shall go forth, suffering pains and afflictions and temptations of every kind; and this that the word might be fulfilled which saith he will take upon him the pains and the sicknesses of his people.

"And he will take upon him death, that he may loose the bands of death which bind his people; and he will take upon him their infirmities, that his bowels may be filled with mercy, according to the flesh, that he may know according to the flesh how to succor his people according to their infirmities.

"Now the Spirit knoweth all things; nevertheless the Son of God suffereth according to the flesh that he might take upon him the sins of his people, that he might blot out their transgressions according to the power of his deliverance; and now behold, this is the testimony which is in me.

"Now I say unto you that ye must repent, and be born again; for the Spirit saith if ye are not born again ye cannot inherit the kingdom of heaven; therefore come and be baptized unto repentance, that ye may be washed from your sins, that ye may have faith on the Lamb of God, who taketh away the sins of the world, who is mighty to save and to cleanse from all unrighteousness." (Alma 7:9-14.)

Alma's final appeal in that city was:

"And now I would that ye should be humble, and be submissive and gentle; easy to be entreated; full of patience and long-suffering; being temperate in all things; being diligent in keeping the commandments of God at all times; asking for whatsoever things ye stand in need, both spiritual and temporal; always returning thanks unto God for whatsoever things ye do receive. And see that ye have faith, hope, and charity, and then ye will always abound in good works.

"And may the Lord bless you, and keep your garments spotless, that ye may at last be brought to sit down with Abraham, Isaac, and Jacob, and the holy prophets who have been ever since the world began, having your garments spotless even as their garments are spotless, in the kingdom of heaven to go no more out."

Chapter 18

AMULEK
JOINS ALMA

One of the most difficult cities on Alma's missionary journey was Ammonihah. There the people refused to listen to him.

"Nevertheless Alma labored much in the spirit, wrestling with God in mighty prayer, that he would pour out his Spirit upon the people who were in the city; that he would also grant that he might baptize them unto repentance.

"Nevertheless, they hardened their hearts, saying unto him: Behold, we know that thou art Alma; and we know that thou art high priest over the church which thou hast established in many parts of the land, according to your tradition; and we are not of thy church, and we do not believe in such foolish traditions."

The people spat on him, railed against him, and said, "We know that because we are not of thy church . . . thou hast no power over us; and thou hast delivered up the judgment-seat to Nephihah; therefore thou art not the chief judge over us." Then they cast him out of the city. Discouraged and sorrowful he walked on his way toward another city named Aaron. Suddenly an angel came to him, saying:

"Blessed art thou, Alma; therefore, lift up thy head and rejoice, for thou hast great cause to rejoice; for thou hast been faithful in keeping the commandments of God from the time which thou receivedst thy first message from him. Behold, I am he that delivered it unto you.

"And behold, I am sent to command thee that thou return to the city of Ammonihah, and preach again unto the people of the city; yea, preach unto them. Yea, say unto them, except they repent the Lord God will destroy them. For behold, they do study at this time that they may destroy the liberty of thy people, (for thus saith the Lord) which is contrary to the statutes, and judgments, and commandments which he has given unto his people."

Alma immediately retraced his steps, entering the city another way. As he entered the gates he met a man and asked him if he would "give an humble servant of God something to eat." To Alma's great surprise the man said: "I am a Nephite, and I know that thou art a holy prophet of God, for thou art the man whom an angel said in a vision: Thou shalt receive. Therefore, go with me into my house and I will impart unto thee of my food; and I know that thou wilt be a blessing unto me and my house.

"And it came to pass that the man received him into his house; and the man was called Amulek; and he brought forth bread and meat and set before Alma. And it came to pass that Alma ate bread and was filled; and he blessed Amulek and his house, and he gave thanks unto God."

After Alma had eaten, he told Amulek that he was Alma, the high priest of the Church, and that he was called to preach repentance to the people of that city. He also told of his fasting preparatory to coming to Ammonihah, and that he was indeed hungry when he met Amulek.

The prophet stayed with Amulek for several days before he began preaching again. "And it came to pass that the people did wax more gross in their iniquities." Amulek joined Alma in his undertaking, "and they were filled with the Holy Ghost.

"And they had power given unto them, insomuch that they could not be confined in dungeons; neither was it possible that any man could slay them; nevertheless they did not exercise their power until they were bound in bands and cast into prison. Now, this was done that the Lord might show forth his power in them.

"And it came to pass that they went forth and began to preach and to prophesy unto the people, according to the spirit and power which the Lord had given them." (Alma 8.)

Chapter 19

AMULEK'S TESTIMONY

The people paid little attention to Alma at first, but when Amulek began to speak, they listened because he was one of them. He identified himself by saying, "I am Amulek; I am the son of Giddonah, who was the son of Ishmael, who was a descendant of Aminadi; and it was the same Aminadi who interpreted the writing which was upon the wall of the temple, which was written by the finger of God.

"And behold, I am also a man of no small reputation among all those who know me; yea, and behold, I have many kindreds and friends, and I have also acquired much riches by the hand of my industry.

"Nevertheless, after all this, I never have known much of the ways of the Lord, and his mysteries and marvelous power. I said I never had known much of these things; but behold, I mistake, for I have seen much of his mysteries and his marvelous power; yea, even in the preservation of the lives of this people.

"Nevertheless, I did harden my heart, for I was called many times and I would not hear; therefore I knew concerning these things, yet I would not know; therefore I went on rebelling against God, in the wickedness of my heart, even until the fourth day of this seventh month, which is in the tenth year of the reign of the judges." (Alma 10:2, 4-6.)

Then he said this surprising thing:

"As I was journeying to see a very near kindred, behold an angel of the Lord appeared unto me and said: Amulek, return to thine own house, for thou shalt feed a prophet of the Lord; yea, a holy man, who is a chosen man of God; for he has fasted many days because of the sins of this people, and he is an hungered, and thou shalt receive him into thy house and feed him, and he shall bless thee and thy house; and the blessing of the Lord shall rest upon thee and thy house.

"And it came to pass that I obeyed the voice of the angel, and returned towards my house. And as I was going thither I found the man whom the angel said unto me: Thou shalt receive into thy house—and behold it was this same man who has been speaking unto you concerning the things of God. And the angel said unto me he is a holy man; wherefore I know he is a holy man because it was said by an angel of God.

"And again, I know that the things whereof he hath testified are true; for behold I say unto you, that as the Lord liveth, even so has he sent his angel to make these things manifest unto me; and this he has done while this Alma hath dwelt at my house."

Amulek told the people how Alma had blessed his family, his wife, his children, and his father, "even all my kindred hath he blessed, and the blessing of the Lord rested upon us."

The people were astonished when they saw that there were two witnesses instead of one. Certain lawyers among them tried to trap the brethren into saying things damaging to themselves, that would form a basis for charges against them, so that they could be jailed, or even slain. But Amulek defended himself by the power of the Holy Spirit. His success in doing so angered the people who charged, "This man doth revile against our laws which are just, and our wise lawyers whom we have selected."

Amulek was not afraid. He cried out mightily to them, saying:

"O ye wicked and perverse generation, why hath Satan got such great hold upon your hearts? Why will ye yield yourselves unto him that he may have power over you, to blind your eyes, that ye will not understand the words which are spoken, according to their truth? For behold, have I testified against your law? Ye do not understand; ye say that I have spoken against your law; but I have not, but I have spoken in favor of your law, to your condemnation.

"And now behold, I say unto you, that the foundation of the destruction of this people is beginning to be laid by the unrighteousness of your lawyers and your judges."

The response from the people was: "Now we know that this man is a child of the devil, for he hath lied unto us; for he hath spoken against our law. And now he says that he has not spoken against it. And again, he has reviled against our lawyers, and our judges." (Alma 10.)

One of the craftiest of the lawyers was a man named Zeezrom, a leader among those accusing Alma and Amulek. He raised the question of whether there is a Christ and whether he shall come. Amulek replied:

"He shall come into the world to redeem his people; and he shall take upon him the transgressions of those who believe on his name; and these are they that shall have eternal life, and salvation cometh to none else.

"Therefore the wicked remain as though there had been no redemption made, except it be the loosing of the bands of death; for behold, the day cometh that all shall rise from the dead and stand before God, and be judged according to their works.

"Now, there is a death which is called a temporal death; and the death of Christ shall loose the bands of this temporal death, that all shall be raised from this temporal death.

"The spirit and the body shall be reunited again in its perfect form; both limb and joint shall be restored to its proper frame, even as we now are at this time; and we shall be brought to stand before God, knowing even as we know now, and have a bright recollection of all our guilt.

"Now, this restoration shall come to all, both old and young, both bond and free, both male and female, both the wicked and the righteous; and even there shall not so much as a hair of their heads be lost; but every thing shall be restored to its perfect frame, as it is now, or in the body, and shall be brought and be arraigned before the bar of Christ the Son, and God the Father, and the Holy Spirit, which is one Eternal God, to be judged according to their works, whether they be good or whether they be evil."

This gave Amulek an opportunity to explain the resurrection:

"Now, behold, I have spoken unto you concerning the death of the mortal body, and also concerning the resurrection of the mortal body. I say unto you that this mortal body is raised to an immortal body, that is from death, even from the first death unto life, that they can die no more; their spirits uniting with their bodies, never to be divided; thus the whole becoming spiritual and immortal, that they can no more see corruption." (Alma 11:40-45.)

When he finished this statement, the people listened in astonishment, but Zeezrom, who had led the attack, now began to tremble.

Seeing how Amulek had silenced Zeezrom, Alma arose and continued the discussion, "for he beheld that Amulek had caught him [Zeezrom] in his lying and deceiving to destroy him." Then, seeing that Zeezrom had begun to tremble "under a consciousness of guilt," Alma bore testimony to the truthfulness of what Amulek had said. He turned to the trembling lawyer and said:

"Now Zeezrom, seeing that thou hast been taken in thy lying and craftiness, for thou hast not lied unto men only but thou hast lied unto God; for behold, he knows all thy thoughts, and thou seest that thy thoughts are made known unto us by his Spirit; and thou seest that we know that thy plan was a very subtle plan, as to the subtlety of the devil, for to lie and to deceive this people that thou mightest set them against us, to revile us and to cast us out—now this was a plan of thine adversary, and he hath exercised his power in thee. Now I would that ye should remember that what I say unto thee I say unto all.

"And behold I say unto you all that this was a snare of the

adversary, which he has laid to catch this people, that he might bring you into subjection unto him, that he might encircle you about with his chains that he might chain you down to everlasting destruction, according to the power of his captivity." (Alma 12:3-6.)

This made Zeezrom tremble more than ever. His heart seemed to soften, and he began to ask questions about the gospel, ceasing his attack upon the brethren.

Chapter 20

ZEEZROM
REPENTS

The wicked lawyer Zeezrom listened as Amulek discoursed on death, the resurrection, and the judgment, and the words made him tremble with fear and to soften even more. Alma went on with his discourse on death and the hereafter:

"This is the thing which I was about to explain. Now we see that Adam did fall by the partaking of the forbidden fruit, according to the word of God; and thus we see, that by his fall, all mankind became a lost and fallen people.

"And now behold, I say unto you that if it had been possible for Adam to have partaken of the fruit of the tree of life at that time, there would have been no death, and the word would have been void, making God a liar, for he said: If thou eat thou shalt surely die.

"And we see that death comes upon mankind, yea, the death which has been spoken of by Amulek, which is the temporal death; nevertheless there was a space granted unto man in which he might repent; therefore this life became a probationary state; a time to prepare to meet God; a time to prepare for that endless state which has been spoken of by us, which is after the resurrection of the dead.

"Now, if it had not been for the plan of redemption, which was laid from the foundation of the world, there could have been no resurrection of the dead; but there was a plan of redemption laid, which shall bring to pass the resurrection of the dead, of which has been spoken.

"And now behold, if it were possible that our first parents could have gone forth and partaken of the tree of life they would have been forever miserable, having no preparatory state; and thus the plan of redemption would have been frustrated, and the word of God would have been void, taking none effect. But behold, it was not so; but it was appointed unto men that they must die; and after death, they must come to judgment, even that same judgment of which we have spoken, which is the end.

"And after God had appointed that these things should come unto man, behold, then he saw that it was expedient that man should know concerning the things whereof he had appointed unto them; therefore he sent angels to converse with them, who caused men to behold of his glory.

"But God did call on men, in the name of his Son, (this being the plan of redemption which was laid) saying: If ye will repent, and harden not your hearts, then will I have mercy upon you, through mine Only Begotten Son; therefore, whosoever repenteth, and hardeneth not his heart, he shall have claim on mercy through mine Only Begotten Son, unto a remission of his sins; and these shall enter into my rest. And whosoever will harden his heart and will do iniquity, behold, I sware in my wrath that he shall not enter into my rest.

"And now, my brethren, behold I say unto you, that if ye will harden your hearts ye shall not enter into the rest of the Lord; therefore your iniquity provoketh him that he sendeth down his wrath upon you as in the first provocation, yea, according to his word in the last provocation as well as the first, to the everlasting destruction of your souls; therefore, according to his word, unto the last death, as well as the first.

"And now, my brethren, seeing we know these things, and they are true, let us repent, and harden not our hearts, that we provoke not the Lord our God to pull down his wrath upon us in these his second commandments which he has given unto us; but let us enter into the rest of God, which is prepared according to his word." (Alma 12:22-37.)

The crowd became increasingly angry as Alma and Amulek preached repentance, and finally they seized the two men and threw them into prison. Now Zeezrom showed his repentance:

"And it came to pass that Zeezrom was astonished at the words which had been spoken; and he also knew concerning the blindness of the minds, which he had caused among the people by his lying words; and his soul began to be harrowed up under a consciousness of his own guilt; yea, he began to be encircled about by the pains of hell.

"And it came to pass that he began to cry unto the people, saying: Behold, I am guilty, and these men are spotless before God. And he began to plead for them from that time forth; but they reviled him, saying: Art thou also possessed with the devil? And they spit upon him, and cast him out from among them, and also all those who believed in the words which had been spoken by Alma and Amulek; and they cast them out, and sent men to cast stones at them." (Alma 14:6-7.)

Chapter 21

BELIEVERS MARTYRED

Alma and Amulek were taken before the chief judge of the land, who was determined to wipe out all effects of their preaching. Some of the people had believed the words of the two brethren, and now they, together with their wives and children, were bound and burned at the stake.

"Whosoever believed or had been taught to believe in the word of God they caused that they should be cast into the fire, and they also brought forth their records which contained the holy scriptures, and cast them into the fire also, that they might be burned and destroyed by fire.

"And it came to pass that they took Alma and Amulek, and carried them forth to the place of martyrdom, that they might witness the destruction of those who were consumed by fire.

"And when Amulek saw the pains of the women and children who were consuming in the fire, he also was pained; and he said unto Alma: How can we witness this awful scene? Therefore let us stretch forth our hands, and exercise the power of God which is in us, and save them from the flames.

"But Alma said unto him: The Spirit constraineth me that I must not stretch forth mine hand; for behold the Lord receiveth them up unto himself, in glory; and he doth suffer that they may do this thing, or that the people may do this thing unto them, according to the hardness of their hearts, that the judgments which he shall exercise upon them in his wrath may be just; and the blood of the innocent shall stand as a witness against them, yea, and cry mightily against them at the last day.

"Now Amulek said unto Alma: Behold, perhaps they will burn us also.

"And Alma said: Be it according to the will of the Lord. But, behold, our work is not finished; therefore they burn us not."

The chief judge came and stood before Alma and Amulek as the flames consumed not only the families of the believers, but all their books as well. He smote the two prophets in the face and said, "After what ye have seen, will ye preach again unto this people, that they shall be cast into a lake of fire and brimstone? Behold, ye see that ye had not power to save those who had been cast into the fire; neither has God saved them because they were of thy faith. And the judge smote them again upon their cheeks, and asked: What say ye for yourselves?"

When Alma and Amulek made no reply, they were again thrown into the prison. Three days later the chief judge and the priests and teachers of their apostate church returned to the prison and questioned the brethren. But again they refused to talk. Their captors visited them again the next day, smiting them again in the face and demanding answers to their questions. They said, "Will ye stand again and judge this people, and condemn our law? If ye have such great power why do ye not deliver yourselves? . . . How shall we look when we are damned?"

The two brethren were left in the prison without food or drink for many days. Then the chief judge of Ammonihah and his lawyers came again. After beating the brethren they said: "If ye have the power of God deliver yourselves from these bands, and then we will believe that the Lord will destroy this people according to your words.

"And it came to pass that they all went forth and smote them, saying the same words, even until the last; and when the last had spoken unto them the power of God was upon Alma and Amulek, and they rose and stood upon their feet.

"And Alma cried, saying: How long shall we suffer these great afflictions, O Lord? O Lord, give us strength according to our faith which is in Christ, even unto deliverance. And they broke the cords with which they were bound; and when the people saw this, they began to flee, for the fear of destruction had come upon them.

"And it came to pass that so great was their fear that they fell to the earth, and did not obtain the outer door of the prison; and the earth shook mightily, and the walls of the prison were rent in twain, so that they fell to the earth; and the chief judge, and the lawyers, and priests, and teachers, who smote upon Alma and Amulek, were slain by the fall thereof."

All in the prison were killed except the two prophets, who walked unharmed from the prison grounds and into the city.

"Now the people having heard a great noise came running together by multitudes to know the cause of it; and when they saw Alma and Amulek coming forth out of the prison, and the walls thereof had fallen to the earth, they were struck with great fear, and fled from the presence of Alma and Amulek even as a goat fleeth with her young from two lions; and thus they did flee from the presence of Alma and Amulek." (Alma 14.)

The Lord now commanded the brethren to leave Ammonihah and go to Sidom. There they found members of the Church; they also discovered Zeezrom, who was sick with a fever. He had thought that because of his own iniquity, Alma and Amulek had been killed. "And this great sin, and his many other sins, did harrow up his mind until it became exceedingly sore, having no deliverance; therefore he began to be scorched with a burning heat."

When he heard that the two brethren were in the city, he sent for them. Alma took him by the hand and said, "Believest thou in the power of Christ unto salvation?

"And he answered and said: Yea, I believe all the words that thou hast taught.

"And Alma said: If thou believest in the redemption of Christ thou canst be healed.

"And he said: Yea, I believe according to thy words.

"And then Alma cried unto the Lord, saying: O Lord our

God, have mercy on this man, and heal him according to his faith which is in Christ.

"And when Alma had said these words, Zeezrom leaped upon his feet, and began to walk; and this was done to the great astonishment of all the people; and the knowledge of this went forth throughout all the land of Sidom.

"And Alma baptized Zeezrom unto the Lord; and he began from that time forth to preach unto the people. And Alma established a church in the land of Sidom, and consecrated priests and teachers in the land, to baptize unto the Lord whosoever were desirous to be baptized."

Many people, having heard of Alma and Amulek, came "from all the region round about Sidom, and were baptized." (Alma 15:1-14.)

Chapter 22

AMMONIHAH IS DESTROYED

The Lord had predicted that Ammonihah and all its evil inhabitants would be destroyed. Alma and Amulek had faithfully delivered this message to the people, but they were completely rejected.

Knowing of the impending destruction, Amulek could not go back to his home or family in that city. The record says that he was rejected by his friends and "his father and his kindred." He had "forsaken all his gold, and silver, and his precious things, which were in the land of Ammonihah, for the word of God."

Amulek now had no place to go. Alma had learned to appreciate his great devotion to the Lord, so "he took Amulek and came over to the land of Zarahemla, and took him to his own house, and did administer unto him in his tribulations, and strengthened him in the Lord." (Alma 15:16-18.)

But then came a cry of war. Peace had prevailed in Zarahemla for a number of years, but now a cry of war was heard throughout the land. The Lamanite armies marched into Nephite territory, but not against Zarahemla. This time they surrounded Ammonihah! Now the word of the Lord was about to be fulfilled.

The Nephites prepared to raise an army to drive the invaders out of their land, but before they could organize their forces, the city of Ammonihah was destroyed, "yea, every living soul of the Ammonihahites was destroyed, and also their great city, which they said God could not destroy, because of its greatness. . . . In one day it was left desolate; and the carcases were mangled by dogs and wild beasts of the wilderness. Nevertheless, after many days their dead bodies were heaped up upon the face of the earth, and they were covered with a shallow covering. And now so great was the scent thereof that the people did not go in to possess the land of Ammonihah for many years. And it was called Desolation of Nehors; for they were of the profession of Nehor, who were slain; and their lands remained desolate.

"And the Lamanites did not come again to war against the Nephites until the fourteenth year of the reign of the judges over the people of Nephi. And thus for three years did the people of Nephi have continual peace in all the land.

"And Alma and Amulek went forth preaching repentance to the people in their temples, and in their sanctuaries, and also in their synagogues, which were built after the manner of the Jews. And as many as would hear their words, unto them they did impart the word of God, without any respect of persons, continually.

"And thus did Alma and Amulek go forth, and also many more who had been chosen for the work, to preach the word throughout all the land. And the establishment of the church became general throughout all the land, in all the region round about, among all the people of the Nephites.

"And there was no inequality among them; the Lord did pour out his Spirit on all the face of the land to prepare the minds of the children of men, or to prepare their hearts to receive the word which should be taught among them at the time of his coming—that they might not be hardened against the word, that they might not be unbelieving, and go on to destruction, but that they might receive the word with joy, and as a branch be grafted into the true vine, that they might enter into the rest of the Lord their God.

"Now those priests who did go forth among the people did preach against all lyings, and deceivings, and envyings, and strifes, and malice, and revilings, and stealing, robbing, plundering, murdering, committing adultery, and all manner of lasciviousness, crying that these things ought not so to be—holding forth things which must shortly come; yea, holding forth the coming of the Son of God, his sufferings and death, and also the resurrection of the dead.

"And many of the people did inquire concerning the place where the Son of God should come; and they were taught that he would appear unto them after his resurrection; and this the people did hear with great joy and gladness.

"And now after the church had been established throughout all the land—having got the victory over the devil, and the word of God being preached in its purity in all the land, and the Lord pouring out his blessings upon the people—thus ended the fourteenth year of the reign of the judges over the people of Nephi." (Alma 16.)

Chapter 23

A JOYOUS REUNION

Many years had passed since Alma, now the high priest of the land, had seen the sons of King Mosiah with whom he had been so friendly earlier in life. They also had been converted when the angel appeared to Alma but they were not stricken down as seriously as was he. In their repentance they desired to serve a mission among the Lamanites in the land of Nephi, and their father, the king, granted them permission. The Lord had told the king that he, the Lord, would preserve their lives while they were among the Lamanites.

Ammon was the leader of these sons of Mosiah. He and his brothers served long among the Lamanites, suffering serious afflictions while doing so, but they were blessed abundantly by the Lord. Thousands of the Lamanites were converted, and now Ammon and his brothers hoped to lead them to Zarahemla, where they would make their homes with other members of the Church.

These Lamanites were so completely converted that they took an oath before God that they would never again take up swords in battle. They had learned that the Nephites were their true brethren, and that they, the Lamanites, had indeed been misled by the false tradition of their fathers, going as far back as the time of Laman and Lemuel, sons of Lehi.

Ammon and his brethren had left their Lamanite converts in the wilderness while they sought permission to bring them in to Zarahemla. Alma also was returning from a journey, and on the road to Zarahemla he met these sons of Mosiah. "And behold, this was a joyful meeting.

"Now the joy of Ammon was so great even that he was full; yea, he was swallowed up in the joy of his God, even to the exhausting of his strength; and he fell again to the earth. Now was not this exceeding joy? Behold, this is joy which none receiveth save it be the truly penitent and humble seeker of happiness. Now the joy of Alma in meeting his brethren was truly great, and also the joy of Aaron, of Omner, and Himni; but behold their joy was not that to exceed their strength.

"And now it came to pass that Alma conducted his brethren back to the land of Zarahemla; even to his own house. And they went and told the chief judge all the things that had happened unto them in the land of Nephi, among their brethren, the Lamanites.

"And it came to pass that the chief judge sent a proclamation throughout all the land, desiring the voice of the people concerning the admitting their brethren, who were the people of Anti-Nephi-Lehi.

"And it came to pass that the voice of the people came, saying: Behold, we will give up the land of Jershon, which is on the east by the sea, which joins the land Bountiful, which is on the south of the land Bountiful; and this land Jershon is the land which we will give unto our brethren for an inheritance."

The Nephites recognized the oath that Ammon's people had taken, pledging that they would never again take up swords in battle, and they therefore allowed Ammon and his brothers to bring their people to Zarahemla.

Alma now accompanied Ammon into the wilderness to bring these faithful converts in to Zarahemla.

"And it came to pass that it did cause great joy among them. And they went down into the land of Jershon, and took possession of the land of Jershon; and they were called by the Nephites the people of Ammon; therefore they were distinguished by that name ever after.

"And they were among the people of Nephi, and also numbered among the people who were of the church of God. And they were also distinguished for their zeal towards God, and also towards men; for they were perfectly honest and upright in all things; and they were firm in the faith of Christ, even unto the end.

"And they did look upon shedding the blood of their brethren with the greatest abhorrence; and they never could be prevailed upon to take up arms against their brethren; and they never did look upon death with any degree of terror, for their hope and views of Christ and the resurrection; therefore, death was swallowed up to them by the victory of Christ over it.

"Therefore, they would suffer death in the most aggravating and distressing manner which could be inflicted by their brethren, before they would take the sword or cimeter to smite them.

"And thus they were a zealous and beloved people, a highly favored people of the Lord." (Alma 27.)

Chapter 24

"O THAT I WERE AN ANGEL"

Sickened by the sins of both his own nation and the Lamanites, and seeing the possibility of great destruction for them if they failed to repent, Alma dedicated himself more than ever to the ministry. He found that preaching of the word "was more powerful even than the sword."

Alma was close to the Lord, and he received revelations frequently for his guidance and comfort. His desire to preach the word of God was overpowering. Lifted up in his great enthusiasm for the work one day he cried out:

"O that I were an angel, and could have the wish of mine heart, that I might go forth and speak with the trump of God, with a voice to shake the earth, and cry repentance unto every people!

"Yea, I would declare unto every soul, as with the voice of thunder, repentance and the plan of redemption, that they should repent and come unto our God, that there might not be more sorrow upon all the face of the earth.

"But behold, I am a man, and do sin in my wish; for I ought to be content with the things which the Lord hath allotted unto me."

Then he continued:

"Why should I desire that I were an angel, that I could speak unto all the ends of the earth? For behold, the Lord doth grant unto all nations, of their own nation and tongue, to teach his word, yea, in wisdom, all that he seeth fit that they should have; therefore we see that the Lord doth counsel in wisdom, according to that which is just and true.

"I know that which the Lord hath commanded me, and I glory in it. I do not glory of myself, but I glory in that which the Lord hath commanded me; yea, and this is my glory, that perhaps I may be an instrument in the hands of God to bring some soul to repentance; and this is my joy.

"And behold, when I see many of my brethren truly penitent, and coming to the Lord their God, then is my soul filled with joy; then do I remember what the Lord has done for me, yea, even that he hath heard my prayer; yea, then do I remember his merciful arm which he extended towards me.

"Yea, and I also remember the captivity of my fathers; for I surely do know that the Lord did deliver them out of bondage, and by this did establish his church; yea, the Lord God, the God of Abraham, the God of Isaac, and the God of Jacob, did deliver them out of bondage. Yea, I have always remembered the captivity of my fathers; and that same God who delivered them out of the hands of the Egyptians did deliver them out of bondage.

"Yea, and that same God did establish his church among them; yea, and that same God hath called me by a holy calling, to preach the word unto this people, and hath given me much success, in the which my joy is full.

"But I do not joy in my own success alone, but my joy is more full because of the success of my brethren, who have been up to the land of Nephi. Behold, they have labored exceedingly, and have brought forth much fruit; and how great shall be their reward! Now, when I think of the success of these my brethren my soul is carried away, even to the separation of it from the body, as it were, so great is my joy.

"And now may God grant unto these, my brethren, that they may sit down in the kingdom of God; yea, and also all those who are the fruit of their labors that they may go no more out, but that they may praise him forever. And may God grant that it may be done according to my words, even as I have spoken. Amen."

Alma had brought hosts of people into the faith, had taught them, had baptized them, had ordained many to the priesthood, and in times of war, had joined with the Nephite armies and fought on the battlefields. He had seen the great losses from these wars, and he hoped to bring peace through the gospel to prevent more bloodshed.

Casualties in these wars were particularly heavy, since all the fighting was hand-to-hand combat with sword and axe, one man to one man; and when one soldier slashed down his opponent, he would go on to another. With this kind of gladiator-like fighting, thousands were killed in a single engagement.

When Alma saw this carnage, and when he afterward heard the mourning of the widows and orphans, the mothers and fathers of the dead, he was sick at heart. He yearned for greater power than he then possessed to preach repentance and faith to his people. Remembering the voice of the angel who had spoken to him and the sons of Mosiah, he knew the power of conversion that accompanied that visitation. Now he and the sons of Mosiah were all in the ministry. The voice of the angel had done its work.

But others needed it. So he wished for angelic power to bring people to Christ. "But," he said, "I am a man, and do sin in my wish: for I ought to be content with the things which the Lord hath allotted unto me." (Alma 29. Italics added.) And so it was.

Chapter 25

ALMA'S DOCTRINES

Above all, Alma was a champion of the Lord Jesus Christ. He knew that the Savior was indeed the Redeemer of the world, the Only Begotten Son of God, who would be born in Palestine, where his atonement would be accomplished.

The Savior spoke personally to Alma. There was a close relationship between this humble servant and his Master. Alma bore his testimony to many thousands, and many thousands were convinced. He testified:

"Not many days hence the Son of God shall come in his glory; and his glory shall be the glory of the Only Begotten of the Father, full of grace, equity, and truth, full of patience, mercy, and long suffering, quick to hear the cries of his people and to answer their prayers. And behold, he cometh to redeem those who will be baptized unto repentance, through faith on his name." (Alma 9:26-27.)

"There is no other way or means whereby man can be saved, only in and through Christ. Behold, he is the life and the light of the world. Behold, he is the word of truth and righteousness." (Alma 38:9.)

Some of Alma's teachings were the following:

Death

"Now there must needs be a space betwixt the time of death and the time of the resurrection. And now I would inquire what becometh of the souls of men from this time of death to the time appointed for the resurrection?

"Now whether there is more than one time appointed for men to rise it mattereth not; for all do not die at once, and this

mattereth not; all is as one day with God, and time only is mea-
sured unto men. Therefore, there is a time appointed unto men
that they shall rise from the dead; and there is a space between
the time of death and the resurrection. And now, concerning
this space of time, what becometh of the souls of men is the
thing which I have inquired diligently of the Lord to know; and
this is the thing of which I do know. And when the time cometh
when all shall rise, then shall they know that God knoweth all
the times which are appointed unto man.

"Now, concerning the state of the soul between death and
the resurrection—Behold, it has been made known unto me by
an angel, that the spirits of all men, as soon as they are departed
from this mortal body, yea, the spirits of all men, whether they
be good or evil, are taken home to that God who gave them life.

"And then shall it come to pass, that the spirits of those who
are righteous are received into a state of happiness, which is
called paradise, a state of rest, a state of peace, where they shall
rest from all their troubles and from all care, and sorrow.

"And then shall it come to pass, that the spirits of the
wicked, yea, who are evil—for behold, they have no part nor
portion of the Spirit of the Lord; for behold, they chose evil
works rather than good; therefore the spirit of the devil did enter
into them, and take possession of their house—and these shall
be cast out into outer darkness; there shall be weeping, and
wailing, and gnashing of teeth, and this because of their own iniquity, being led captive by the will of the devil.

"Now this is the state of the souls of the wicked, yea, in
darkness, and a state of awful, fearful looking for the fiery in-
dignation of the wrath of God upon them; thus they remain in
this state, as well as the righteous in paradise, until the time of
their resurrection." (Alma 40:6-14.)

Resurrection

"There is a space between death and the resurrection of the
body, and a state of the soul in happiness or in misery until the

time which is appointed of God that the dead shall come forth, and be reunited, both soul and body, and be brought to stand before God, and be judged according to their works.

"Yea, this bringeth about the restoration of those things of which has been spoken by the mouths of the prophets. The soul shall be restored to the body, and the body to the soul; yea, and every limb and joint shall be restored to its body; yea, even a hair of the head shall not be lost; but all things shall be restored to their proper and perfect frame.

"And now, my son, this is the restoration of which has been spoken by the mouths of the prophets—and then shall the righteous shine forth in the kingdom of God.

"But behold, an awful death cometh upon the wicked; for they die as to things pertaining to things of righteousness; for they are unclean, and no unclean thing can inherit the kingdom of God; but they are cast out, and consigned to partake of the fruits of their labors or their works, which have been evil; and they drink the dregs of a bitter cup." (Alma 40:21-26.)

Immorality

"Know ye not, my son, that these things are an abomination in the sight of the Lord; yea, most abominable above all sins save it be the shedding of innocent blood or denying the Holy Ghost?

"For behold, if ye deny the Holy Ghost when it once has had place in you, and ye know that ye deny it, behold, this is a sin which is unpardonable; yea, and whosoever murdereth against the light and knowledge of God, it is not easy for him to obtain forgiveness; yea, I say unto you, my son, that it is not easy for him to obtain a forgiveness.

"And now, my son, I would to God that ye had not been guilty of so great a crime. I would not dwell upon your crimes, to harrow up your soul, if it were not for your good. But behold, ye cannot hide your crimes from God; and except ye repent they will stand as a testimony against you at the last day." (Alma 39:5-8.)

Humility

"See that ye are not lifted up unto pride; yea, see that ye do not boast in your own wisdom, nor of your much strength. Use boldness, but not overbearance; and also see that ye bridle all your passions, that ye may be filled with love; see that ye refrain from idleness.

"Do not pray as the Zoramites do, for ye have seen that they pray to be heard of men, and to be praised for their wisdom. Do not say: O God, I thank thee that we are better than our brethren; but rather say: O Lord, forgive my unworthiness, and remember my brethren in mercy—yea, acknowledge your unworthiness before God at all times." (Alma 38:11-14.)

Prayer

"Yea, and cry unto God for all thy support; yea, let all thy doings be unto the Lord, and whithersoever thou goest let it be in the Lord; yea, let thy thoughts be directed unto the Lord; yea, let the affections of thy heart be placed upon the Lord forever.

"Counsel with the Lord in all thy doings, and he will direct thee for good; yea, when thou liest down at night lie down unto the Lord, that he may watch over you in your sleep; and when thou risest in the morning let thy heart be full of thanks unto God; and if ye do these things, ye shall be lifted up at the last day." (Alma 37:36-37.)

Devotion

"Preach unto them repentance, and faith on the Lord Jesus Christ; teach them to humble themselves and to be meek and lowly in heart; teach them to withstand every temptation of the devil, with their faith on the Lord Jesus Christ. Teach them to never be weary of good works, but to be meek and lowly in heart; for such shall find rest to their souls.

"O, remember, my son, and learn wisdom in thy youth; yea, learn in thy youth to keep the commandments of God." (Alma 37:33-35.)

Amulek on Prayer

Therefore may God grant unto you, my brethren, that ye may begin to exercise your faith unto repentance, that ye begin to call upon his holy name, that he would have mercy upon you;

Yea, cry unto him for mercy; for he is mighty to save.

Yea, humble yourselves, and continue in prayer unto him.

Cry unto him when ye are in your fields, yea, over all your flocks.

Cry unto him in your houses, yea, over all your household, both morning, mid-day, and evening.

Yea, cry unto him against the power of your enemies.

Yea, cry unto him against the devil, who is an enemy to all righteousness.

Cry unto him over the crops of your fields, that ye may prosper in them.

Cry over the flocks of your fields, that they may increase.

But this is not all; ye must pour out your souls in your closets, and your secret places, and in your wilderness.

Yea, and when you do not cry unto the Lord, let your hearts be full, drawn out in prayer unto him continually for your welfare, and also for the welfare of those who are around you.

And now behold, my beloved brethren, I say unto you, do not suppose that this is all; for after ye have done all these things, if ye turn away the needy, and the naked, and visit not the sick and afflicted, and impart of your substance, if ye have, to those who stand in need—I say unto you, if ye do not any of these things, behold, your prayer is vain, and availeth you nothing, and ye are as hypocrites who do deny the faith.

Therefore, if ye do not remember to be charitable, ye are as dross, which the refiners do cast out, (it being of no worth) and is trodden under foot of men.

And now, my brethren, I would that, after ye have received so many witnesses, seeing that the holy scriptures testify of these things, ye come forth and bring fruit unto repentance.

(Alma 34:17-30.)

Obedience

"Yea, he that truly humbleth himself, and repenteth of his sins, and endureth to the end, the same shall be blessed—yea, much more blessed than they who are compelled to be humble because of their exceeding poverty.

"Therefore, blessed are they who humble themselves without being compelled to be humble; or rather, in other words, blessed is he that believeth in the word of God, and is baptized without stubbornness of heart, yea, without being brought to know the word, or even compelled to know, before they will believe." (Alma 32:15-16.)

"And now, my son, I would that ye should understand that these things are not without a shadow; for as our fathers were slothful to give heed to this compass (now these things were temporal) they did not prosper; even so it is with things which are spiritual.

For behold, it is as easy to give heed to the word of Christ, which will point to you a straight course to eternal bliss, as it was for our fathers to give heed to this compass, which would point unto them a straight course to the promised land.

"And now I say, is there not a type in this thing? For just as surely as this director did bring our fathers, by following its course, to the promised land, shall the words of Christ, if we follow their course, carry us beyond this vale of sorrow into a far better land of promise." (Alma 37:43-45.)

Diligence

"O my son, do not let us be slothful because of the easiness of the way; for so was it with our fathers; for so was it prepared for them, that if they would look they might live; even so it is with us. The way is prepared, and if we will look we may live forever." (Alma 34:46.)

The Fall of Adam

"Adam did fall by the partaking of the forbidden fruit, according to the word of God; and thus we see, that by his fall, all mankind became a lost and fallen people.

"And now behold, I say unto you that if it had been possible for Adam to have partaken of the fruit of the tree of life at that time, there would have been no death, and the word would have been void, making God a liar, for he said: If thou eat thou shalt surely die.

"And we see that death comes upon mankind, yea, the death which has been spoken of by Amulek, which is the temporal death; nevertheless there was a space granted unto man in which he might repent; therefore this life became a probationary state; a time to prepare to meet God; a time to prepare for that endless state which has been spoken of by us, which is after the resurrection of the dead.

"Now, if it had not been for the plan of redemption, which was laid from the foundation of the world, there could have been no resurrection of the dead; but there was a plan of redemption laid, which shall bring to pass the resurrection of the dead, of which has been spoken.

"And now behold, if it were possible that our first parents could have gone forth and partaken of the tree of life they would have been forever miserable, having no preparatory state; and thus the plan of redemption would have been frustrated, and the word of God would have been void, taking none effect.

"But behold, it was not so; but it was appointed unto men that they must die; and after death, they must come to judgment, even that same judgment of which we have spoken, which is the end." (Alma 12:22-27.)

The Second Death

"If our hearts have been hardened, yea, if we have hardened our hearts against the word, insomuch that it has not been found in us, then will our state be awful, for then we shall be condemned. For our words will condemn us, yea, all our works will condemn us; we shall not be found spotless; and our thoughts will also condemn us; and in this awful state we shall not dare to look up to our God; and we would fain be glad if we could command the rocks and the mountains to fall upon us to hide us from his presence.

"But this cannot be; we must come forth and stand before him in his glory, and in his power, and in his might, majesty, and dominion, and acknowledge to our everlasting shame that all his judgments are just; that he is just in all his works, and that he is merciful unto the children of men, and that he has all power to save every man that believeth on his name and bringeth forth fruit meet for repentance.

"And now behold, I say unto you then cometh a death, even a second death, which is a spiritual death; then is a time that whosoever dieth in his sins, as to a temporal death, shall also die a spiritual death; yea, he shall die as to things pertaining unto righteousness.

"Then is the time when their torments shall be as a lake of fire and brimstone, whose flame ascendeth up forever and ever; and then is the time that they shall be chained down to an everlasting destruction, according to the power and captivity of Satan, he having subjected them according to his will.

"Then, I say unto you, they shall be as though there had been no redemption made; for they cannot be redeemed according to God's justice; and they cannot die, seeing there is no more corruption." (Alma 12:13-18.)

Volunteer Service

"Now Alma said unto him: Thou knowest that we do not glut ourselves upon the labors of this people; for behold I have labored even from the commencement of the reign of the judges until now, with mine own hands for my support, notwithstanding my many travels round about the land to declare the word of God unto my people.

"And notwithstanding the many labors which I have performed in the church, I have never received so much as even one senine for my labor; neither has any of my brethren, save it were in the judgment-seat; and then we have received only according to law for our time.

"And now, if we do not receive anything for our labors in the church, what doth it profit us to labor in the church save it were to declare the truth, that we may have rejoicings in the joy of our brethren?" (Alma 30:32-34.)

Faith

"And now as I said concerning faith—faith is not to have a perfect knowledge of things; therefore if ye have faith ye hope for things which are not seen, which are true. . . .

"But if ye will nourish the word, yea, nourish the tree as it beginneth to grow, by your faith with great diligence, and with patience, looking forward to the fruit thereof, it shall take root; and behold it shall be a tree springing up unto everlasting life.

"And because of your diligence and your faith and your patience with the word in nourishing it, that it may take root in you, behold, by and by ye shall pluck the fruit thereof, which is most precious, which is sweet above all that is sweet, and which is white above all that is white, yea, and pure above all that is pure; and ye shall feast upon this fruit even until ye are filled, that ye hunger not, neither shall ye thirst.

"Then, my brethren, ye shall reap the rewards of your faith, and your diligence, and patience, and long-suffering, waiting for the tree to bring forth fruit unto you." (Alma 32:21, 41-43.)

Chapter 26

THE CHALLENGE OF KORIHOR

Korihor was an anti-Christ who lived about 74 B.C. He admitted having been trained in his apostasy by the devil. He came into the city of Zarahemla and began to denounce the prophecies that had been made concerning the coming of the Messiah. Since there was freedom of speech among the Nephites, there was no law to stop him.

He cried out: "Why do ye look for a Christ? For no man can know of anything which is to come. Behold, these things which ye call prophecies, which ye say are handed down by holy prophets, behold, they are foolish traditions of your fathers. How do ye know of their surety? Behold, ye cannot know of things which ye do not see; therefore ye cannot know that there shall be a Christ. Ye look forward and say that ye see a remission of your sins. But behold, it is the effect of a frenzied mind; and this derangement of your minds comes because of the traditions of your fathers, which lead you away into a belief of things which are not so." (Alma 30:13-16.)

Korihor led away the hearts of many, the record says, "causing them to lift up their heads in their wickedness, yea, leading away many women, and also men, to commit whoredoms—telling them that when a man was dead, that was the end thereof."

He next went over to the land of Jershon, where the people of Ammon were more faithful and wise than the Nephites. They bound him and carried him before Ammon, their high priest.

Ammon ordered Korihor "carried out of the land." Then Korihor went to the city of Gideon, where he was bound and carried before Giddonah, the high priest and the chief judge of that land. The high priest asked, "Why do ye go about pervert-ing the ways of the Lord? Why do ye teach this people that there shall be no Christ, to interrupt their rejoicings? Why do ye speak against all the prophecies of the holy prophets?"

Korihor replied, "Because I do not teach the foolish tradi-tions of your fathers, and because I do not teach this people to bind themselves down under the foolish ordinances and perfor-mances which are laid down by ancient priests, to usurp power and authority over them, to keep them in ignorance, that they may not lift up their heads, but be brought down according to thy words.

"Ye say that this people is a free people. Behold, I say they are in bondage. Ye say that those ancient prophecies are true. Behold, I say that ye do not know that they are true.

"Ye say that this people is a guilty and a fallen people, be-cause of the transgression of a parent. Behold, I say that a child is not guilty because of its parents.

"And ye also say that Christ shall come. But behold, I say that ye do not know that there shall be a Christ. And ye say also that he shall be slain for the sins of the world—and thus ye lead away this people after the foolish traditions of your fathers, and according to your own desires; and ye keep them down, even as it were in bondage, that ye may glut yourselves with the labors of their hands, that they durst not look up with boldness, and that they durst not enjoy their rights and privileges."

"Now when the high priest and the chief judge saw the hard-ness of his heart, yea, when they saw that he would revile even against God, they would not make any reply to his words; but they caused that he should be bound; and they delivered him up into the hands of the officers, and sent him to the land of Zarahemla, that he might be brought before Alma, and the chief judge who was governor over all the land."

When he was brought before Alma, Korihor proceeded as he had done in Gideon, "and did revile against the priests and teachers, accusing them of leading away the people after the silly traditions of their fathers, for the sake of glutting on the labors of the people."

Alma replied: "Thou knowest that we do not glut ourselves upon the labors of this people; for behold I have labored even from the commencement of the reign of the judges until now, with mine own hands for my support, notwithstanding my many travels round about the land to declare the word of God unto my people."

Then Alma asked Korihor, "Believest thou that there is a God?"

Korihor said, "Nay."

Alma continued: "Will ye deny again that there is a God, and also deny the Christ? For behold, I say unto you, I know there is a God, and also that Christ shall come. And now what evidence have ye that there is no God, or that Christ cometh not? I say unto you that ye have none, save it be your word only. But, behold, I have all things as a testimony that these things are true; and ye also have all things as a testimony unto you that they are true; and will ye deny them? Believest thou that these things are true?

"Behold, I know that thou believest, but thou art possessed with a lying spirit, and ye have put off the Spirit of God that it may have no place in you; but the devil has power over you, and he doth carry you about, working devices that he may destroy the children of God."

When Korihor asked for a sign, Alma said that he had had signs enough. However, Korihor insisted, and again he denied both God and Christ, saying that he would not believe without a sign.

Alma told him, "This will I give unto thee for a sign, that thou shalt be struck dumb, according to my words; and I say, that in the name of God, ye shall be struck dumb, that ye shall no more have utterance."

When Alma had said these words, Korihor was struck dumb.

When the chief judge saw this, he wrote to Korihor, "Art thou convinced of the power of God? In whom did ye desire that Alma should show forth his sign? Would ye that he should afflict others, to show unto thee a sign? Behold, he has showed unto you a sign; and now will ye dispute more?"

Korihor replied in writing, "I know that I am dumb, for I cannot speak; and I know that nothing save it were the power of God could bring this upon me; yea, and I always knew that there was a God. But behold, the devil hath deceived me; for he appeared unto me in the form of an angel, and said unto me: Go and reclaim this people, for they have all gone astray after an unknown God. And he said unto me: There is no God; yea, and he taught me that which I should say. And I have taught his words; and I taught them because they were pleasing unto the carnal mind; and I taught them, even until I had much success, insomuch that I verily believed that they were true; and for this cause I withstood the truth, even until I have brought this great curse upon me."

Korihor asked that the curse be taken from him, but Alma refused. Korihor then went about from door to door, begging for food. As he did so "he was run upon and trodden down, even until he was dead."

"Now the knowledge of what had happened unto Korihor was immediately published throughout all the land; yea, the proclamation was sent forth by the chief judge to all the people in the land, declaring unto those who had believed in the words of Korihor that they must speedily repent, lest the same judgments would come unto them.

"And it came to pass that they were all convinced of the wickedness of Korihor; therefore they were all converted again unto the Lord; and this put an end to the iniquity after the manner of Korihor." (Alma 30.)

Chapter 27

THE ZORAMITE APOSTASY

One of the most difficult apostate groups Alma had to deal with was the Zoramites, who practiced idolatry. These people lived in the land of Antionum, east of the land of Zarahemla, near the seashore. The Nephites feared that the Zoramites would join with the Lamanites in attacking them, and this worried Alma.

"And now, as the preaching of the word had a great tendency to lead the people to do that which was just—yea, it had had more powerful effect upon the minds of the people than the sword, or anything else, which had happened unto them—therefore Alma thought it was expedient that they should try the virtue of the word of God."

Alma took two of his sons, two of the sons of Mosiah (Aaron and Omner), and also Ammon, Amulek, and Zeezrom with him on a journey to the Zoramites, hoping to convert them. The Zoramites were dissenters from the Nephites. They already knew some of the gospel teachings, but Zoram had introduced idolatry and immoral practices.

Alma and his company were astonished at what they found when they arrived in Antionum. They had never seen the kind of worship that existed there. The Zoramites had built up in the center of their synagogue "a place for standing, which was high above the head; and the top thereof would only admit one person.

"Therefore, whosoever desired to worship must go forth and stand upon the top thereof, and stretch forth his hands towards heaven, and cry with a loud voice, saying:

"Holy, holy God; we believe that thou art God, and we believe that thou art holy, and that thou wast a spirit, and that thou art a spirit, and that thou wilt be a spirit forever.

"Holy God, we believe that thou hast separated us from our brethren; and we do not believe in the tradition of our brethren, which was handed down to them by the childishness of their fathers; but we believe that thou hast elected us to be thy holy children; and also thou hast made it known unto us that there shall be no Christ.

"But thou art the same yesterday, today, and forever; and thou hast elected us that we shall be saved, whilst all around us are elected to be cast by thy wrath down to hell; for the which holiness, O God, we thank thee; and we also thank thee that thou hast elected us, that we may not be led away after the foolish traditions of our brethren, which doth bind them down to a belief of Christ, which doth lead their hearts to wander far from thee, our God.

"And again we thank thee, O God, that we are a chosen and a holy people. Amen."

Every man in the congregation went forward and offered the identical prayer with his hands stretched forth to heaven, "thanking their God that they were chosen of him, and that he did not lead them away after the tradition of their brethren, and that their hearts were not stolen away to believe in things to come, which they knew nothing about."

After the worship was over, the people returned to their homes, never speaking of God again until they reassembled in the synagogues.

Alma himself bowed in prayer and said:

"Behold, O God, they cry unto thee, and yet their hearts are swallowed up in their pride. Behold, O God, they cry unto thee with their mouths, while they are puffed up, even to greatness, with the vain things of the world.

"Behold, O my God, their costly apparel, and their ringlets, and their bracelets, and their ornaments of gold, and all their precious things which they are ornamented with; and behold, their hearts are set upon them, and yet they cry unto thee and say—We thank thee, O God, for we are a chosen people unto thee, while others shall perish.

"Yea, and they say that thou hast made it known unto them that there shall be no Christ."

Then he prayed that he and his brethren would have success in teaching these people. (Alma 31.)

Alma and his companions began their work, going first to the poor and humble of the city. They spoke in some of the synagogues as well as in the streets. Before long they were cast out of the synagogues, as were the poorer people who listened to them and who had allowed them to preach there.

One day Alma spoke from a hill known as Onihah. A large multitude of the poor people followed him there and complained about being forced out of synagogues that they themselves had built. He told them, "I behold that ye are lowly in heart; and if so, blessed are ye. Behold thy brother hath said, What shall we do?—for we are cast out of our synagogues, that we cannot worship our God. Behold I say unto you, do ye suppose that ye cannot worship God save it be in your synagogues only? And moreover, I would ask, do ye suppose that ye must not worship God only once in a week?

"I say unto you, it is well that ye are cast out of your synagogues, that ye may be humble, and that ye may learn wisdom; for it is necessary that ye should learn wisdom; for it is because that ye are cast out, that ye are despised of your brethren because of your exceeding poverty, that ye are brought to a lowliness of heart; for ye are necessarily brought to be humble.

"And now, because ye are compelled to be humble blessed are ye; for a man sometimes, if he is compelled to be humble, seeketh repentance; and now surely, whosoever repenteth shall find mercy; and he that findeth mercy and endureth to the end the same shall be saved.

"And now, as I said unto you, that because ye were compelled to be humble ye were blessed, do ye not suppose that they are more blessed who truly humble themselves because of the word? Yea, he that truly humbleth himself, and repenteth of his sins, and endureth to the end, the same shall be blessed—yea, much more blessed than they who are compelled to be humble because of their exceeding poverty.

"Therefore, blessed are they who humble themselves without being compelled to be humble; or rather, in other words, blessed is he that believeth in the word of God, and is baptized without stubbornness of heart, yea, without being brought to know the word, or even compelled to know, before they will believe." (Alma 32:1-16.)

Alma then began to preach to the Zoramites concerning Christ, the Son of God. He quoted two former prophets, Zenos and Zenock, both of them testifying of Christ.

When Amulek arose to speak, he also testified of Christ. He too quoted Zenos and Zenoch concerning the Savior, and then he said, "And now, behold, I will testify unto you of myself that these things are true. Behold, I say unto you, that I do know that Christ shall come among the children of men, to take upon him the transgressions of his people, and that he shall atone for the sins of the world; for the Lord God hath spoken it."

He explained that there must be one great and last sacrifice, "and then shall there be, or it is expedient there should be, a stop to the shedding of blood; then shall the law of Moses be fulfilled; yea, it shall be all fulfilled, every jot and tittle, and none shall have passed away.

"And behold, this is the whole meaning of the law, every whit pointing to that great and last sacrifice; and that great and last sacrifice will be the Son of God, yea, infinite and eternal. And thus he shall bring salvation to all those who shall believe on his name; this being the intent of this last sacrifice, to bring about the bowels of mercy, which overpowereth justice, and bringeth about means unto men that they may have faith unto repentance." (Alma 34:1-15.)

Teaching the people to pray over their families, their fields, and their flocks and herds, Amulek called on them to repent, saying, "Behold, this life is the time for men to prepare to meet God; yea, behold the day of this life is the day for men to perform their labors."

He explained why they must not postpone their repentance: "For behold, if ye have procrastinated the day of your repentance even until death, behold, ye have become subjected to the spirit of the devil, and he doth seal you his; therefore, the Spirit of the Lord hath withdrawn from you, and hath no place in you, and the devil hath all power over you; and this is the final state of the wicked." (Alma 34:32-35.)

Chapter 28

CORIANTON'S INIQUITY

As earnestly as Alma and his brethren had labored, they were seriously handicapped by one of their own number—Corianton, Alma's son.

At first Corianton participated in the ministry, but he did so in a spirit of boasting. Then he left the other brethren and slipped over to a nearby city of the Lamanites to consort with a harlot named Isabel.

Alma rebuked his son for this wickedness. "Behold, O my son," the father said, "how great iniquity ye brought upon the Zoramites; for when they saw your conduct they would not believe in my words."

"And this is not all, my son," Alma continued. "Thou didst do that which was grievous unto me; for thou didst forsake the ministry, and did go over into the land of Siron among the borders of the Lamanites, after the harlot Isabel. Yea, she did steal away the hearts of many; but this was no excuse for thee, my son. Thou shouldst have tended to the ministry wherewith thou wast entrusted.

"Know ye not, my son, that these things are an abomination in the sight of the Lord; yea, most abominable above all sins save it be the shedding of innocent blood or denying the Holy Ghost? For behold, if ye deny the Holy Ghost when it once has had place in you, and ye know that ye deny it, behold, this is a sin which is unpardonable; yea, and whosoever murdereth against the light and knowledge of God, it is not easy for him to obtain forgiveness; yea, I say unto you, my son, that it is not easy for him to obtain a forgiveness.

"And now, my son, I would to God that ye had not been

guilty of so great a crime. I would not dwell upon your crimes, to harrow up your soul, if it were not for your good. But behold, ye cannot hide your crimes from God; and except ye repent they will stand as a testimony against you at the last day."

Alma loved his son and sought earnestly to save him, and so he said, "Now my son, I would that ye should repent and forsake your sins, and go no more after the lusts of your eyes, but cross yourself in all these things; for except ye do this ye can in nowise inherit the kingdom of God. Oh, remember, and take it upon you, and cross yourself in these things.

"And I command you to take it upon you to counsel with your elder brothers in your undertakings; for behold, thou art in thy youth, and ye stand in need to be nourished by your brothers. And give heed to their counsel.

"Suffer not yourself to be led away by any vain or foolish thing; suffer not the devil to lead your heart again after those wicked harlots."

Alma then turned to teaching his son about Christ, on whom all salvation rests:

"And now, my son, I would say somewhat unto you concerning the coming of Christ. Behold, I say unto you, that it is he that surely shall come to take away the sins of the world; yea, he cometh to declare glad tidings of salvation unto his people.

"And now, my son, this was the ministry unto which ye were called, to declare these glad tidings unto this people, to prepare their minds; or rather that salvation might come unto them, that they may prepare the minds of their children to hear the word at the time of his coming.

"And now I will ease your mind somewhat on this subject. Behold, you marvel why these things should be known so long beforehand. Behold, I say unto you, is not a soul at this time as precious unto God as a soul will be at the time of his coming? Is it not as necessary that the plan of redemption should be made known unto this people as well as unto their children? Is it not as easy at this time for the Lord to send his angel to declare these glad tidings unto us as unto our children, or as after the time of his coming?" (Alma 39:1-19.)

Alma also taught another son, Shiblon, who had been true to the ministry but still was young and in need of guidance. In contrast to his talk with Corianton, he said to Shiblon, "I say unto you, my son, that I have had great joy in thee already, because of thy faithfulness and thy diligence, and thy patience and thy long-suffering among the people of the Zoramites. For I know that thou wast in bonds; yea, and I also know that thou wast stoned for the word's sake; and thou didst bear all these things with patience because the Lord was with thee; and now thou knowest that the Lord did deliver thee."

He told Shiblon of his own conversion by the appearance of an angel who called him to repentance. After reviewing this experience he said to Shiblon, "And now, my son, I have told you this that ye may learn wisdom, that ye may learn of me that there is no other way or means whereby man can be saved, only in and through Christ. Behold, he is the life and the light of the world. Behold, he is the word of truth and righteousness.

"And now, as ye have begun to teach the word even so I would that ye should continue to teach; and I would that ye would be diligent and temperate in all things. See that ye are not lifted up unto pride; yea, see that ye do not boast in your own wisdom, nor of your much strength. Use boldness, but not over-bearance; and also see that ye bridle all your passions, that ye may be filled with love; see that ye refrain from idleness.

"Do not pray as the Zoramites do, for ye have seen that they pray to be heard of men, and to be praised for their wisdom. Do not say: O God, I thank thee that we are better than our brethren; but rather say: O Lord, forgive my unworthiness, and remember my brethren in mercy—yea, acknowledge your unworthiness before God at all times." (Alma 38:3-14.)

Chapter 29

HELAMAN THE FAITHFUL

Alma also told Helaman of his own sinful past and of his great conversion to Christ. He said, "If I had not been born of God I should not have known these things; but God has, by the mouth of his holy angel, made these things known unto me, not of any worthiness of myself." (Alma 36:5.)

Bearing strong testimony of the goodness of God, he promised Helaman abundant blessings if he would keep the commandments.

"But behold, my son, this is not all; for ye ought to know as I do know, that inasmuch as ye shall keep the commandments of God ye shall prosper in the land; and ye ought to know also, that inasmuch as ye will not keep the commandments of God ye shall be cut off from his presence. Now this is according to his word.

"O remember, remember, my son Helaman, how strict are the commandments of God. And he said: If ye will keep my commandments ye shall prosper in the land—but if ye keep not his commandments ye shall be cut off from his presence." (Alma 36:30; 37:13.)

Alma then made Helaman the custodian of all the sacred records that had been kept so carefully and handed down by previous prophets.

"And now remember, my son, that God has entrusted you with these things, which are sacred, which he has kept sacred, and also which he will keep and preserve for a wise purpose in him, that he may show forth his power unto future generations.

"And now behold, I tell you by the spirit of prophecy, that if ye transgress the commandments of God, behold, these things which are sacred shall be taken away from you by the power of God, and ye shall be delivered up unto Satan, that he may sift you as chaff before the wind.

"But if ye keep the commandments of God, and do with these things which are sacred according to that which the Lord doth command you, (for you must appeal unto the Lord for all things whatsoever ye must do with them) behold, no power of earth or hell can take them from you, for God is powerful to the fulfilling of all his words. For he will fulfil all his promises which he shall make unto you, for he has fulfilled his promises which he has made unto our fathers. For he promised unto them that he would reserve these things for a wise purpose in him, that he might show forth his power unto future generations."

Alma then explained to Helaman about the twenty-four plates that had been taken to Mosiah, who translated them. Those are the plates that provided the Book of Ether for us. Said Alma:

"And now, I will speak unto you concerning those twenty-four plates, that ye keep them, that the mysteries and the works of darkness, and their secret works, or the secret works of those people who have been destroyed, may be manifest unto this people; yea, all their murders, and robbings, and their plunderings, and all their wickedness and abominations, may be made manifest unto this people; yea, and that ye preserve these interpreters.

"For behold, the Lord saw that his people began to work in darkness, yea, work secret murders and abominations; therefore the Lord said, if they did not repent they should be destroyed from off the face of the earth." (Alma 37:14-22.)

He said further, "Counsel with the Lord in all thy doings, and he will direct thee for good; yea, when thou liest down at night lie down unto the Lord, that he may watch over you in your sleep; and when thou risest in the morning let thy heart be full of thanks unto God; and if ye do these things, ye shall be lifted up at the last day." (Alma 37:37.)

There was one more thing that Alma needed to tell Helaman:

"And now, my son, I have somewhat to say concerning the thing which our fathers call a ball, or director—or our fathers called it Liahona, which is, being interpreted, a compass; and the Lord prepared it.

"And behold, there cannot any man work after the manner of so curious a workmanship. And behold, it was prepared to show unto our fathers the course which they should travel in the wilderness. And it did work for them according to their faith in God; therefore, if they had faith to believe that God could cause that those spindles should point the way they should go, behold, it was done; therefore they had this miracle, and also many other miracles wrought by the power of God, day by day.

"Nevertheless, because those miracles were worked by small means it did show unto them marvelous works. They were slothful, and forgot to exercise their faith and diligence and then those marvelous works ceased, and they did not progress in their journey; therefore, they tarried in the wilderness, or did not travel a direct course, and were afflicted with hunger and thirst, because of their transgressions."

And then he continued: "And now I say, is there not a type in this thing? For just as surely as this director did bring our fathers, by following its course, to the promised land, shall the words of Christ, if we follow their course, carry us beyond this vale of sorrow into a far better land of promise."

Alma concluded: "And now, my son, see that ye take care of these sacred things, yea, see that ye look to God and live. Go unto this people and declare the word, and be sober. My son, farewell." (Alma 37:37-47.)

Chapter 30

THE ZORAMITES DECLARE WAR

Many of the more righteous Zoramites, including those who were poorer and more humble, listened to Alma and were converted. But most of the people resisted. Certain of their leaders became angry to the point of urging war against the Nephites. The scripture says that the Zoramites actually became Lamanites (Alma 43:4), and the combined group prepared for war.

"And it came to pass that the Lamanites came with their thousands; and they came into the land of Antionum, which is the land of the Zoramites; and a man by the name of Zerahemnah was their leader.

"And now, as the Amalekites were of a more wicked and murderous disposition than the Lamanites were, in and of themselves, therefore, Zerahemnah appointed chief captains over the Lamanites, and they were all Amalekites and Zoramites.

"Now this he did that he might preserve their hatred towards the Nephites, that he might bring them into subjection to the accomplishment of his designs. For behold, his designs were to stir up the Lamanites to anger against the Nephites; this he did that he might usurp great power over them, and also that he might gain power over the Nephites by bringing them into bondage." (Alma 43:5-8.)

The Nephites organized to meet this new invasion. Knowing that the Lamanites had a deep hatred for the people of Ammon, formerly of their own kind who had been converted by Ammon and brought to Zarahemla, the Nephites made plans to protect them from attack. The people of Ammon, therefore, moved out of the land of Jershon, which had been given them for homes, and went to Melek. The Nephite army took their place in Jershon and prepared their defense.

Although the people of Ammon had pledged not to take up the sword, they did furnish the Nephite army with large portions of their needed supplies.

The Nephites appointed a twenty-five-year-old man to be their commanding general. His name was Moroni, and he proved to be a military genius in the defense of the people of God. A mighty champion of liberty, he was devoted to the Lord.

The Lamanites were armed with only their swords and bows and arrows. Moroni dressed his men in thick clothing with breastplates and arm shields to prevent their arms from being cut off in combat. He also provided helmets to cover their heads.

The commander of the Zoramites and Lamanites was a vicious man named Zerahemnah.

"Now the army of Zerahemnah was not prepared with any such thing; they had only their swords and their cimeters, their bows and their arrows, their stones and their slings; and they were naked, save it were a skin which was girded about their loins; yea, all were naked, save it were the Zoramites and the Amalekites; but they were not armed with breastplates, nor shields—therefore, they were exceedingly afraid of the armies of the Nephites because of their armor, notwithstanding their number being so much greater than the Nephites.

"Behold, now it came to pass that they durst not come against the Nephites in the borders of Jershon; therefore they departed out of the land of Antionum into the wilderness, and took their journey round about in the wilderness, away by the head of the river Sidon, that they might come into the land of Manti and take possession of the land; for they did not suppose that the armies of Moroni would know whither they had gone."

Moroni sent spies after them, "and Moroni, also, knowing of the prophecies of Alma, sent certain men unto him, desiring him that he should inquire of the Lord whither the armies of the Nephites should go to defend themselves against the Lamanites.

"And it came to pass that the word of the Lord came unto Alma, and Alma informed the messengers of Moroni, that the armies of the Lamanites were marching round about in the wilderness, that they might come over into the land of Manti, that they might commence an attack upon the weaker part of the people. And those messengers went and delivered the message unto Moroni." (Alma 43:1-24.)

In the battles that followed, thousands of men were slain. The armies of Moroni surrounded the enemy, and when Zerahemnah's men discovered this, they were "struck with terror." Moroni, seeing how frightened they were, then commanded his men to hold up further attack.

"And it came to pass that they did stop and withdrew a pace from them. And Moroni said unto Zerahemnah: Behold, Zerahemnah, that we do not desire to be men of blood. Ye know that ye are in our hands, yet we do not desire to slay you.

"Behold, we have not come out to battle against you that we might shed your blood for power; neither do we desire to bring any one to the yoke of bondage. But this is the very cause for which ye have come against us; yea, and ye are angry with us because of our religion.

"But now, ye behold that the Lord is with us; and ye behold that he has delivered you into our hands. And now I would that ye should understand that this is done unto us because of our religion and our faith in Christ. And now ye see that ye cannot destroy this our faith.

"Now ye see that this is the true faith of God; yea, ye see that God will support, and keep, and preserve us, so long as we are faithful unto him, and unto our faith, and our religion; and never will the Lord suffer that we shall be destroyed except we should fall into transgression and deny our faith.

"And now, Zerahemnah, I command you, in the name of

that all-powerful God, who has strengthened our arms that we have gained power over you, by our faith, by our religion, and by our rites of worship, and by our church, and by the sacred support which we owe to our wives and our children, by that liberty which binds us to our lands and our country; yea, and also by the maintenance of the sacred word of God, to which we owe all our happiness; and by all that is most dear unto us—yea, and this is not all; I command you by all the desires which ye have for life, that ye deliver up your weapons of war unto us, and we will seek not your blood, but we will spare your lives, if ye will go your way and come not again to war against us.

"And now, if ye do not this, behold, ye are in our hands, and I will command my men that they shall fall upon you, and inflict the wounds of death in your bodies, that ye may become extinct; and then we will see who shall have power over this people; yea, we will see who shall be brought into bondage.

"And now it came to pass that when Zerahemnah had heard these sayings he came forth and delivered up his sword and his cimeter, and his bow into the hands of Moroni, and said unto him: Behold, here are our weapons of war; we will deliver them up unto you, but we will not suffer ourselves to take an oath unto you, which we know that we shall break, and also our children; but take our weapons of war, and suffer that we may depart into the wilderness; otherwise we will retain our swords, and we will perish or conquer.

"Behold, we are not of your faith; we do not believe that it is God that has delivered us into your hands; but we believe that it is your cunning that has preserved you from our swords. Behold, it is your breastplates and your shields that have preserved you.

"And now when Zerahemnah had made an end of speaking these words, Moroni returned the sword and the weapons of war, which he had received, unto Zerahemnah, saying: Behold, we will end the conflict.

"Now I cannot recall the words which I have spoken, there-

fore as the Lord liveth, ye shall not depart except ye depart with
an oath that ye will not return again against us to war. Now as ye
are in our hands we will spill your blood upon the ground, or ye
shall submit to the conditions which I have proposed.

"And now when Moroni had said these words, Zerahemnah
retained his sword, and he was angry with Moroni, and he
rushed forward that he might slay Moroni; but as he raised his
sword, behold, one of Moroni's soldiers smote it even to the
earth, and it broke by the hilt; and he also smote Zerahemnah
that he took off his scalp and it fell to the earth. And Zerahemnah withdrew from before them into the midst of his soldiers.

"And it came to pass that the soldier who stood by, who
smote off the scalp of Zerahemnah, took up the scalp from off
the ground by the hair, and laid it upon the point of his sword,
and stretched it forth unto them, saying unto them with a loud
voice:

"Even as this scalp has fallen to the earth, which is the scalp
of your chief, so shall ye fall to the earth except ye will deliver
up your weapons of war and depart with a covenant of peace.

"Now there were many, when they heard these words and
saw the scalp which was upon the sword, that were struck with
fear; and many came forth and threw down their weapons of war
at the feet of Moroni, and entered into a covenant of peace. And
as many as entered into a covenant they suffered to depart into
the wilderness.

"Now it came to pass that Zerahemnah was exceedingly
wroth, and he did stir up the remainder of his soldiers to anger,
to contend more powerfully against the Nephites.

"And now Moroni was angry, because of the stubbornness
of the Lamanites; therefore he commanded his people that they
should fall upon them and slay them. And it came to pass that
they began to slay them; yea, and the Lamanites did contend
with their swords and their might.

"But behold, their naked skins and their bare heads were ex-
posed to the sharp swords of the Nephites; yea, behold they

were pierced and smitten, yea, and did fall exceedingly fast before the swords of the Nephites; and they began to be swept down, even as the soldier of Moroni had prophesied.

"Now Zerahemnah, when he saw that they were all about to be destroyed, cried mightily unto Moroni, promising that he would covenant and also his people with them, if they would spare the remainder of their lives, that they never would come to war again against them.

"And it came to pass that Moroni caused that the work of death should cease again among the people. And he took the weapons of war from the Lamanites; and after they had entered into a covenant with him of peace they were suffered to depart into the wilderness.

"Now the number of their dead was not numbered because of the greatness of the number; yea, the number of their dead was exceedingly great, both on the Nephites and on the Lamanites.

"And it came to pass that they did cast their dead into the waters of Sidon, and they have gone forth and are buried in the depths of the sea.

"And the armies of the Nephites, or of Moroni, returned and came to their houses and their lands." (Alma 44:1-23.)

Chapter 31

ALMA
IS TAKEN

Alma sensed that he was nearing the end of his mortal mission. Knowing that faithful Helaman would take over the work, Alma called his son before him. He must reassure himself of Helaman's faithfulness, so he asked him, "Believest thou the words which I spake unto thee concerning those records which have been kept?"

Helaman replied, "Yea, I believe."

Alma said again, "Believest thou in Jesus Christ, who shall come?"

"Yea, I believe all the words which thou hast spoken."

"Will ye keep my commandments?"

Helaman said, "Yea, I will keep thy commandments with all my heart."

Then Alma told him, "Blessed art thou; and the Lord shall prosper thee in this land."

Alma had a prediction to leave with his son:

"But behold, I have somewhat to prophesy unto thee; but what I prophesy unto thee ye shall not make known; yea, what I prophesy unto thee shall not be made known, even until the prophecy is fulfilled; therefore write the words which I shall say.

"And these are the words: Behold, I perceive that this very people, the Nephites, according to the spirit of revelation which is in me, in four hundred years from the time that Jesus Christ shall manifest himself unto them, shall dwindle in unbelief.

"Yea, and then shall they see wars and pestilences, yea, famines and bloodshed, even until the people of Nephi shall become extinct—yea, and this because they shall dwindle in unbelief and fall into the works of darkness, and lasciviousness, and all manner of iniquities; yea, I say unto you, that because they shall sin against so great light and knowledge, yea, I say unto you, that from that day, even the fourth generation shall not all pass away before this great iniquity shall come.

"And when that great day cometh, behold, the time very soon cometh that those who are now, or the seed of those who are now numbered among the people of Nephi, shall no more be numbered among the people of Nephi.

"But whosoever remaineth, and is not destroyed in that great and dreadful day, shall be numbered among the Lamanites, and shall become like unto them, all, save it be a few who shall be called the disciples of the Lord; and them shall the Lamanites pursue even until they shall become extinct. And now, because of iniquity, this prophecy shall be fulfilled."

Alma now blessed Helaman and his other sons, and the earth for the sake of righteous people. But he added: "Thus saith the Lord God—Cursed shall be the land, yea, this land, unto every nation, kindred, tongue, and people, unto destruction, which do wickedly, when they are fully ripe; and as I have said so shall it be; for this is the cursing and the blessing of God upon the land, for the Lord cannot look upon sin with the least degree of allowance."

This was Alma's last pronouncement. "And now, when Alma had said these words he blessed the church, yea, all those who should stand fast in the faith from that time henceforth.

"And when Alma had done this he departed out of the land of Zarahemla, as if to go into the land of Melek. And it came to pass that he was never heard of more; as to his death or burial we know not of.

"Behold, this we know, that he was a righteous man; and the saying went abroad in the church that he was taken up by the Spirit, or buried by the hand of the Lord, even as Moses. But behold, the scriptures saith the Lord took Moses unto himself; and we suppose that he has also received Alma in the spirit, unto himself; therefore, for this cause we know nothing concerning his death and burial." (Alma 45:1-19.)

INDEX

Aaron: son of Mosiah, 39; was high priest, 53; is reunited with Alma, 83-84; Korihor is brought before, 98; goes with Alma to face Zoramites, 102; people of, go to Melek, 114

Aaron, city of, 66

Abinadi: lived in King Noah's colony, 7; called people to repentance, 7, 10-11; receives revelation from the Lord, 7-8; is forced into hiding, 8; is told to resume preaching repentance, 10; describes afflications to come upon Noah's people, 10-11; is taken before Noah, 11; is imprisoned by Noah, 12; preaches on the law of Moses, 12-13; teachings of, parallel King James Version, 14; was familiar with brass plates, 15; words of, parallel those in King James Version, 15-17; teachings of, compared with those of Joseph Smith, 19-20; on salvation for sin, 19; on the resurrection, 19-21; is condemned to death by Noah, 22-23; martyrdom of, 23

Adultery, laws concerning, 50-51

Alma the elder: priest of Noah, 22; had been evil but repents, 25; officiates at baptism of followers, 25; is ordained by father to be high priest, 25; teaches words of Abinadi, 26; teaches near waters of Mormon, 26; baptizes Helam and 204 persons, 27-28; ordains priests, 28; commands people to share substance, 28-29; departs with people into wilderness, 30; is asked to be king but refuses, 30-31; is appointed high priest and establishes church, 31; people of, are oppressed by Amulon, 32; pours out heart to the Lord, 33; and his people are delivered through faith, 33; establishes branches of church, 33-34; is head of church under Mosiah, 35; dissenters are brought before, 35; seeks help from the Lord in governing church, 36; dies at age eighty-two, 47

Alma the younger: preached about Christ's mission, 2-3; was wicked and idolatrous, 39; angel appears to, 39-40; is struck dumb, 40; recovers speech and repents, 41-42; begins to take over ministry of father, 43; appointed first chief judge, 46; receives brass plates from King Mosiah, 46; teaches concerning higher priesthood, 53-55; slays Amlici, 60; assigns office of chief judge to Nephihah, 61; missionary journey of, 62; teaches about Christ, 63-64,